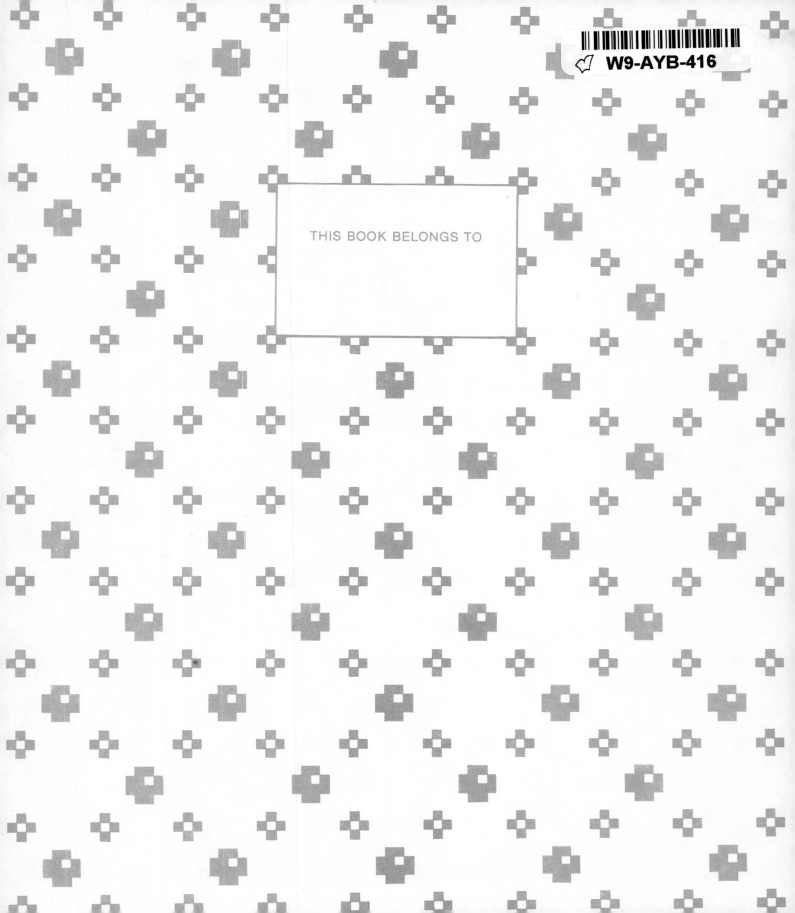

THIS BOOK BELONGS TO

COUNTRY CROSS-STITCH DESIGNS

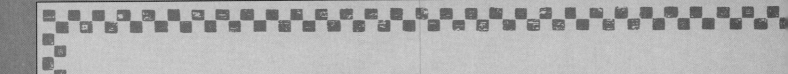

COUNTRY CROSS-STITCH DESIGNS

By Ellen Stouffer

Sedgewood® Press

New York, N.Y.

For Sedgewood® Press
Director: ELIZABETH P. RICE
Manager, Product Development:
    PATRICIA VAN NOTE
Editorial Project Manager: CONNIE SCHRADER
Production Manager: BILL ROSE

Photographer: RYNE HAZEN
The homes of Neil and Cherril Grose and Will and
Diana Allison were used for the photography in this
book. We appreciate their trust and cooperation.

ISBN: 0-696-02335-0
First Printing 1989
Library of Congress Catalog number: 89-061411

Published by Sedgewood® Press

Distributed by Meredith Corporation,
Des Moines, Iowa.

10 9 8 7 6 5 4 3 2 1

Imagine an 1848 Gothic cottage surrounded by colorful flower gardens and a variety of trees. Here, whitetail deer, Canada geese and multitudes of cats roam freely, occasionally stopping to observe their owner at work. Enter the private world of Ellen Stouffer.

In 1968, Ellen married William P. Stouffer and thus joined a Quaker family. She lives with her husband in Wabash, Indiana, in a house that was home to Bill's father and grandfather before him.

The family's 255 years of rich heritage in America includes farmers, artists and clockmakers. Incorporating this legacy with her own unique style, Ellen creates memorable stories about faith, love, prayer, honesty and work.

Ellen's works reflect a part of her that she describes as "gossamer wings"—the love of lace, flowers and pretty things. But more importantly, they are an extension of her desire to share God's promise of comfort and hope.

Outside her home, Ellen teaches elementary art, which fosters some of the youthful spirit seen in her designs. The poems and stories so well-known to her and her pupils inspired a menagerie of fairytale costumes in the chapter entitled "Meagan's Storybook Styles."

Ellen Stouffer's samplers are a special part of her deep faith that she loves to share with friends and strangers alike. Now, transformed into imaginative and useful items, you can enjoy her magical style through the art of cross-stitch.

Dear Cross-Stitcher:

We're delighted you have selected Ellen Stouffer's *Country Cross-Stitch Designs: An American Sampler 1990*. This engaging and happy book is the second in a series of annual publications, just for people who love cross-stitch.

A checkered border motif frames each page, embracing the charming designs, careful chartings, detailed and clear instructions and wonderful drawings, which combine to capture the purity and innocence of "country." Also included is a superb collection of witty sayings, personal reminiscences, and little gems of folklore wisdom — all perfect to ponder, as you stitch your favorite design.

Sedgewood Press strives to bring you the very highest quality craft books, with fine designs, unusual uses for projects, clear instructions, and full color photographs showing each project. We're very proud of *Country Cross-Stitch Designs*, and we hope you'll use it happily to create your own projects.

Sincerely,

Patricia Van Note
Manager, Product Development
Sedgewood® Press

CONTENTS

One can almost smell the fragrant aroma of this lovely springtime sampler. Surprise someone with this May basket and bring cheer to their home all year long.

SPRING BOUQUET

Stitched on ivory damask Aida 14 over one thread, the finished design size is 10⅞" × 15⅝". The fabric was cut 17" × 22".

FABRIC	DESIGN SIZES
Aida 11	13⅞" × 19⅞"
Aida 18	8½" × 12"
Hardanger 22	7" × 10"

Step One: Cross-stitch (two strands)

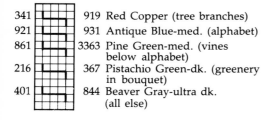

ANCHOR		DMC (used for sample)
891		676 Old Gold-lt.
306		725 Topaz
324		922 Copper-lt.
349		921 Copper
341		919 Red Copper
4146		950 Sportsman Flesh-lt.
868		758 Terra-Cotta-lt.
5975		356 Terra-Cotta-med.
9		760 Salmon
11		3328 Salmon-med.
13		347 Salmon-dk.
968		778 Antique Mauve-lt.
894		223 Shell Pink-med.
869		3042 Antique Violet-lt.
871		3041 Antique Violet-med.
920		932 Antique Blue-lt.
921		931 Antique Blue-med.
266		3347 Yellow Green-med.
861		3363 Pine Green-med.
215		320 Pistachio Green-med.
216		367 Pistachio Green-dk.
378		841 Beige Brown-lt.
380		839 Beige Brown-dk.

Step Two: Backstitch (one strand)

341		919 Red Copper (tree branches)
921		931 Antique Blue-med. (alphabet)
861		3363 Pine Green-med. (vines below alphabet)
216		367 Pistachio Green-dk. (greenery in bouquet)
401		844 Beaver Gray-ultra dk. (all else)

Step Three: French Knots (one strand)

401		844 Beaver Gray-ultra dk.

Stitch Count: 153 × 219

COUNTRY CLOCK

Stitched on cream Belfast Linen 32 over two threads, the finished design size is 6¼″ × 4¼″. The fabric was cut 12″ × 10″. Insert in clock following manufacturer's instructions.

Step One: Cross-stitch (two strands)

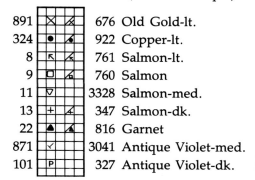

ANCHOR		DMC (used for sample)
891		676 Old Gold-lt.
324		922 Copper-lt.
8		761 Salmon-lt.
9		760 Salmon
11		3328 Salmon-med.
13		347 Salmon-dk.
22		816 Garnet
871		3041 Antique Violet-med.
101		327 Antique Violet-dk.

Stitch Count: 101 × 67

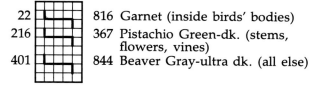

158		828 Blue Ultra-vy. lt.
779		926 Slate Green-dk.
922		930 Antique Blue-dk.
843		3364 Pine Green
216		367 Pistachio Green-dk.
900		3024 Brown Gray-vy. dk.
8581		3023 Brown Gray-lt.

Step Two: Backstitch (one strand)

22		816 Garnet (inside birds' bodies)
216		367 Pistachio Green-dk. (stems, flowers, vines)
401		844 Beaver Gray-ultra dk. (all else)

Step Three: French Knots (one strand)

401		844 Beaver Gray-ultra dk.

FLORAL BOX

The floral design was taken from **Spring Bouquet**. Stitch on driftwood Belfast Linen 32 over two threads with the design centered; see photo. The finished design size is 6½" × 4⅜". The fabric was cut 18" × 16". The stitch count is 104 × 70. Insert in box following manufacturer's instructions.

PAPER ALPHABET

The alphabet and hearts were taken from **Spring Bouquet**. Stitched on craft brown Perforated Paper 14 over one, the finished design size is 9" × 10½". Use one 12" × 18" sheet of paper. Trace pattern for block onto paper thirty times. Center and stitch each letter inside a block. Then stitch four blocks with one heart in each. The small heart is found next to the alphabet. Cut out each block. Frame between two 13" × 15" pieces of glass with blocks ½" apart and one heart block in each corner.

MARY HAD A LITTLE LAMB

Mary's little lamb is sure to follow with Mary dressed in this smart and simple school smock. Stitched with lacy cross-stitch hearts, this dress is perfect for both school and play. *See instructions on page 129.*

From her pallet of images, an artist paints her own rendition of the ABCs. The alphabet has never been more colorful as she blends rich country colors with favorite scripture.

LETTERS FROM THE HEART

Stitched on cream Belfast Linen 32 over two threads, the finished design size is 15⅞″ × 12⅞″. The fabric was cut 22″ × 19″.

FABRIC	DESIGN SIZES
Aida 11	23⅛″ × 18¾″
Aida 14	18¼″ × 14¾″
Aida 18	14⅛″ × 11½″
Hardanger 22	11⅝″ × 9⅜″

Step One: Cross-stitch (two strands)

ANCHOR   DMC (used for sample)

1	White
891	676 Old Gold-lt.
323	722 Orange Spice-lt.
324	721 Orange Spice-med.
326	720 Orange Spice-dk.
349	921 Copper
11	3328 Salmon-med.
13	347 Salmon-dk.
869	3042 Antique Violet-lt.
871	3041 Antique Violet-med.
900	928 Slate Green-lt.
920	932 Antique Blue-lt.
921	931 Antique Blue-med.
922	930 Antique Blue-dk.
843	3364 Pine Green
216	367 Pistachio Green-dk.
885	739 Tan-ultra vy. lt.
378	841 Beige Brown-lt.
380	839 Beige Brown-dk.
401	844 Beaver Gray-ultra dk.

Step Two: Backstitch (one strand)

401	844 Beaver Gray-ultra dk.

Step Three: French Knots (one strand)

401	844 Beaver Gray-ultra dk.

Let us draw near with a sincere heart

Hebrews 10:22

Stitch Count: 255 × 207

A

B

C

you are our letter written in our hearts. 2 Corinthians 3:2

THREE LETTERS

The designs were taken from **Letters from the Heart**. Stitched on cream Belfast Linen 32 over two threads, the finished design size is 1½" × 3½". The fabric was cut 6" × 8" for each.

Artist Ellen Stouffer presents twelve new works of art each year in a continuing series of calendars. They are available in bookstores nationwide. Here, a favorite one is framed with the initials of a friend.

WIZARD OF OZ

Dorothy is off to see the Wizard in her jumper decked with a basket full of cross-stitch apples and trimmed with a tiny flower border. After endless adventures down the yellow brick road, Dorothy's glittering red shoes take her to the best of all places—home. Her dress instructions are on page 132.

BULLETIN BOARD

Stitched on oatmeal Floba 25 over two threads, the finished design size is 20⅜″ × 16½″. The fabric was cut 27″ × 23″. Stitch the checkerboard/star border and the outline for three boxes on the left and three on the right. Then stitch motifs for A, B and C vertically on the left and X, Y and Z on the right; see photo.

MATERIALS
Completed cross-stitch on oatmeal Floba 25
One frame with a 22⅞″ × 18½″ opening
Two 22⅞″ × 18½″ pieces of Foam-Cor for mat and
   backing
One 12¼″ × 12″ piece of ⅛″–deep cork
Brass craft pins (½″)
Double-sided tape
Brown craft paper
Frame hanging kit
Glue

DIRECTIONS

1. Cut a 12¼″ × 12″ window in the center of one piece of Foam-Cor, making certain the corners are right angles. Center over the wrong side of design piece. Trace the outline of the window. Make a second line 1½″ inside the first line. Cut on the second pencil line. Clip each corner at a 45-degree angle between the cutting line and the window line.

2. On the back of the mat, place a piece of tape near the top center edge of the window. Repeat on bottom and sides. Reposition the mat, aligning the window edge with the pencil line. Fold the fabric over the edge. Place pins in the edge, following the grain of the fabric. Secure with tape. Keeping fabric taut, repeat along the bottom edge and then the sides.

3. Repeat the process with the tape and pins on the outside edge. Place the mat in the frame. Place the second piece of Foam-Cor behind the mat. Secure both in the frame.

4. Glue the cork in the mat window.

5. Cut a piece of brown craft paper that is larger than the back of the frame. Glue the paper to the frame. Trim. With a spray bottle filled with water, lightly spray the paper. Allow to dry. (The paper will shrink.)

6. With frame hanging kit, twist one eye-screw into one side of the frame 7″ from the top. Repeat on other side. Cut hanging wire 28″ long. Adjust length if necessary. Thread and secure according to assembly instructions.

SEWING BASKET

Stitched on cream Belfast Linen 32 over two threads, the fabric was cut 6" × 4" for each pocket. The letters H, N, S and T were stitched with each motif placed ¼" to the right of the letter. Cut three 4" × 3" pieces for the checkerboard pieces. Center and stitch two rows of checkerboard 3" long for each.

MATERIALS

Completed cross-stitch for four pockets on cream Belfast Linen 32; matching thread
Completed cross-stitch for three pieces of checkerboard on cream Belfast Linen 32
½ yard of unstitched cream Belfast Linen 32
⅜ yard of matching fabric for lining
⅜ yard of polyester fleece
One basket with flat bottom*
1¼ yards of medium cording
Tracing paper for pattern
Dressmakers' pen

DIRECTIONS

All seam allowances are ¼".

1. Trim design pieces for pockets to 5½" × 3½" with design centered. Trim checkerboard pieces to 3" × 1½". From lining material, cut four 5½" × 3½" pieces for pockets and three 3" × 1½" pieces for checkerboard.

2. With right sides together, stitch top and sides of pocket design pieces and lining. Then stitch the long edges of checkerboard pieces and lining. Turn. Set aside.

3. Make pattern for inside bottom of basket, adding ¼" for seam allowance. Fold pattern into quarters to check for symmetry. From pattern, cut linen, lining, and fleece.

4. Measure outside edge of basket bottom pattern and add 2". Cut 1"–wide bias from unstitched linen piecing as needed to equal measurement. Make corded piping from bias strip.

5. Measure depth of basket and add ½" for seam allowances. Cut a piece of linen this width and twice the length of the corded piping, piecing as needed. Stitch gathering threads in both long edges and gather to fit around sides of basket. Disperse stitching fullness evenly and secure 1½" below top and 1½" above bottom. Cut fleece and lining to fit the gathered side panel.

6. Center and pin pockets on side panel 2½" apart. Pin checkerboard strips horizontally between pockets 1¼" above bottom edge of fabric. Stitch edges of pockets over checkerboard pieces, securing checkerboard pieces in seams.

7. Stitch corded piping to right side of linen bottom piece. Pin fleece to wrong side of side panel. With right sides together, stitch side panel/fleece to bottom piece on the stitching line of piping, securing fleece in seam.

8. With right sides together, stitch bottom lining to side panel lining. Slide over linen with right sides together. Stitch around top of side panel and lining, leaving an opening for turning. Turn. Slipstitch opening closed. Slipstitch finished piece to bottom and sides of basket as needed.

* The basket used for this model is a 13" × 16" oval. All quantities for materials are based on this size. Adjust yours as needed to fit your basket.

An artist retells the familiar story of Noah and his ark with the stroke of her brush. At the first sign of rain, the animals parade two-by-two into the ark to begin their nautical journey.

NOAH'S ARK

Stitched on ivory damask Aida 14 over one thread the finished design size is 16¼″ × 13⅛″. The fabric was cut 23″ × 20″.

FABRIC	DESIGN SIZES
Aida 11	20⅝″ × 16⅝″
Aida 18	12⅝″ × 10⅛″
Hardanger 22	10⅜″ × 8⅜″

Step One: Cross-stitch (two strands)

ANCHOR   DMC (used for sample)

	1	White
926		Ecru
306	725	Topaz
891	676	Old Gold-lt.
890	729	Old Gold-med.
323	722	Orange Spice-lt.
326	720	Orange Spice-dk.
890	729	Old Gold-med. (one strand)
324	922	Copper-lt. (one strand)
324	922	Copper-lt.
339	920	Copper-med.
341	919	Red Copper
9	760	Salmon
11	3328	Salmon-med.
13	347	Salmon-dk.
869	3042	Antique Violet-lt.
871	3041	Antique Violet-med.
920	932	Antique Blue-lt.
921	931	Antique Blue-med.
900	928	Slate Green-lt.
851	924	Slate Green-vy. dk.
843	3364	Pine Green
215	320	Pistachio Green-med.
246	319	Pistachio Green-vy. dk.
942	738	Tan-vy. lt.
378	841	Beige Brown-lt.

380	839	Beige Brown-dk.
8581	3023	Brown Gray-lt.
401	844	Beaver Gray-ultra dk.

Step Two: Backstitch (one strand)

246	319	Pistachio Green-vy. dk. (all branches, stems)
401	844	Beaver Gray-ultra dk. (all else)

Step Three: French Knots (one strand)

246	319	Pistachio Green-vy. dk.
401	844	Beaver Gray-ultra dk.

by faith we stand
thy words giveth light

Stitch Count: 227 × 183

36

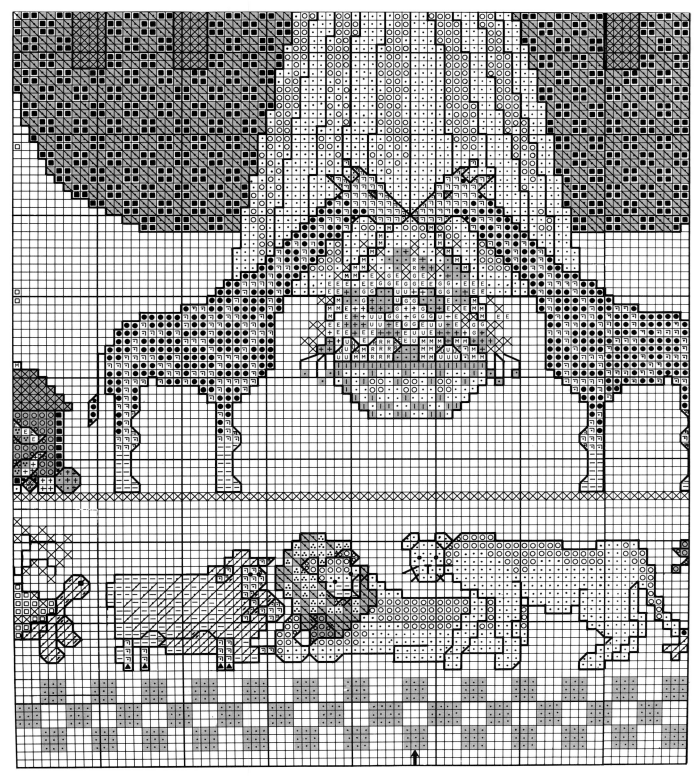

MATERIALS for one sachet

Completed cross-stitch on Jobelan 28; matching
   thread
Paper for pattern
Stuffing
Potpourri
One antique button

DIRECTIONS

All seam allowances are ¼".

1. Make pattern. Place pattern over design with animal's feet toward the corner. Cut out, noting straight of fabric on pattern.

2. Fold ¼" on all edges to wrong side; baste. Fold all corners to the center. Slipstitch edges together for three seams. Stuff moderately, adding potpourri. Slipstitch the fourth seam closed.

3. Sew button to center of sachet.

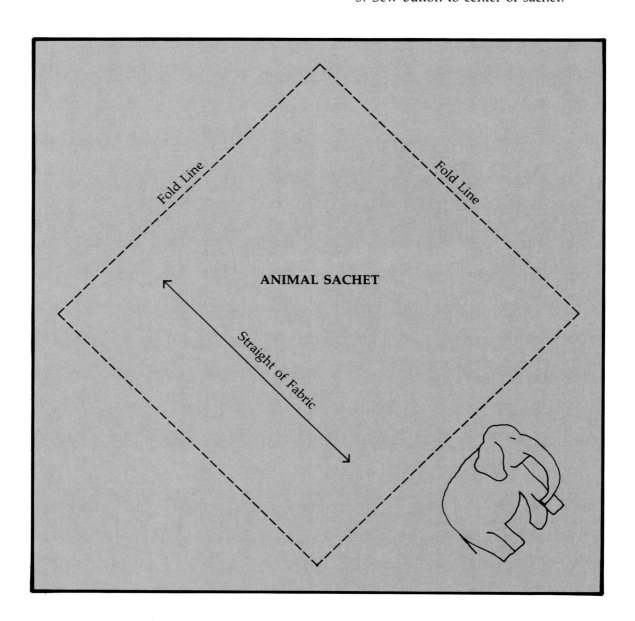

HIGH CHAIR SEAT

The animal borders are taken from **Noah's Ark**. Stitched on ivory Belfast Linen 32 over two threads, the finished design size is 10″ × 10¼″. The fabric was cut 18″ × 18″. For the top edge, the center of the flower in front of the sheep is 3″ from the edge of the fabric. Stitch all four edges, beginning with the rabbits on the left, the tigers on the right and the lions on the bottom. Each design row will be about 8½″ long and use full motifs. Stitch a shell in each corner.

LITTLE ROCKING CHAIR

The design is the center ark and rainbow on **Noah's Ark**. Stitched on celery green Linda 27 over two threads, the finished design size is 8⅝″ × 8⅞″. The fabric was cut 20″ × 20″ with the design centered; see photo. The stitch count is 115 × 121. Insert in rocking chair following manufacturer's instructions.

THREE ANIMAL SACHETS

The animal motifs were taken from **Noah's Ark**. The zebra was stitched on tan Jobelan 28; the sheep was stitched on delicate teal Jobelan 28; and the elephant was stitched on ivory Jobelan 28 all over two threads. The finished design size for the largest animal is 1⅝″ × 1¼″. The fabric was cut 11″ × 11″ for each sachet. Center and stitch the motif with the animal's feet 2″ from the bottom edge. The stitch counts are 22 × 18 for the zebra, 20 × 15 for the sheep and 18 × 16 for the elephant.

A magical childhood rich in
wonderful memories is
recreated with teddy bears,
puppy dogs, baby dolls and
shiny trinkets.

BLESS THIS HOUSE

Stitched on ivory damask Aida 14 over one thread, the finished design size is 17⅝" × 14⅜". The fabric was cut 24" × 21".

FABRIC	DESIGN SIZES
Aida 11	22⅜" × 18¼"
Aida 18	13⅝" × 11⅛"
Hardanger 22	11⅛" × 9⅛"

Step One: Cross-stitch (two strands)

ANCHOR   DMC (used for sample)

926	· ⁄	Ecru
891	○ ⁄	676 Old Gold-lt.
890	✕ ⁄	729 Old Gold-med.
324	I ⁄	721 Orange Spice-med.
326	▽ ⁄	720 Orange Spice-dk.
349	= ⁄	921 Copper
341	▲ ⁄	919 Red Copper
9	○ ⁄	760 Salmon
13	⸬	347 Salmon-dk.
920	◇ ⁄	932 Antique Blue-lt.
922	· ⁄	930 Antique Blue-dk.
843	∴ ⁄	3364 Pine Green
216	● ⁄	367 Pistachio Green-dk.
373	▫	422 Hazel Nut Brown-lt.
309	△ ⁄	435 Brown-vy. lt.
371	✕ ⁄	433 Brown-med.
380	⅄	839 Beige Brown-dk.
8581	+ ⁄	3023 Brown Gray-lt.
401	■	844 Beaver Gray-ultra dk.

Step Two: Backstitch (one strand)

922		930 Antique Blue-dk. (alphabet)
401		844 Beaver Gray-ultra dk. (all else)

Step Three: French Knots (one strand)

401	●	844 Beaver Gray-ultra dk.

May this house to every guest
Be a place of cheer and rest.

Stitch Count: 246 × 201

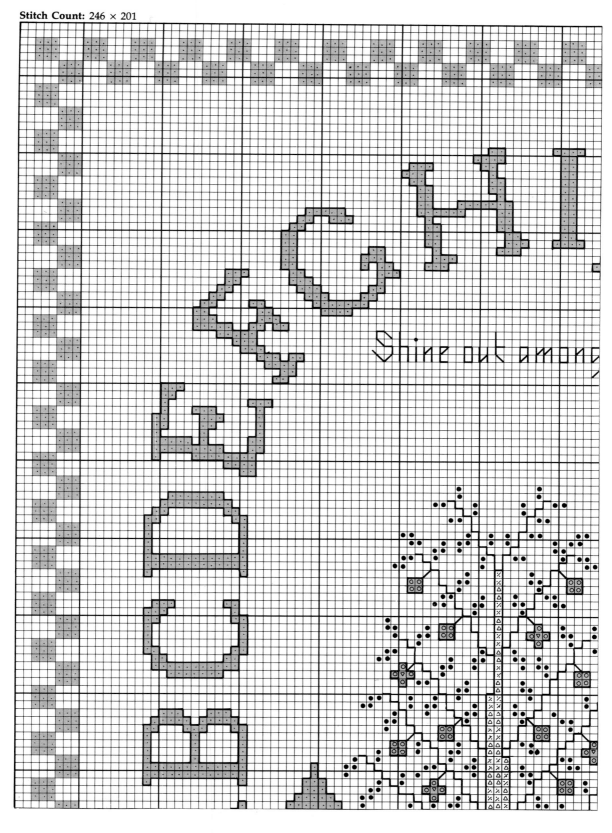

them like beacon lights   Holding o

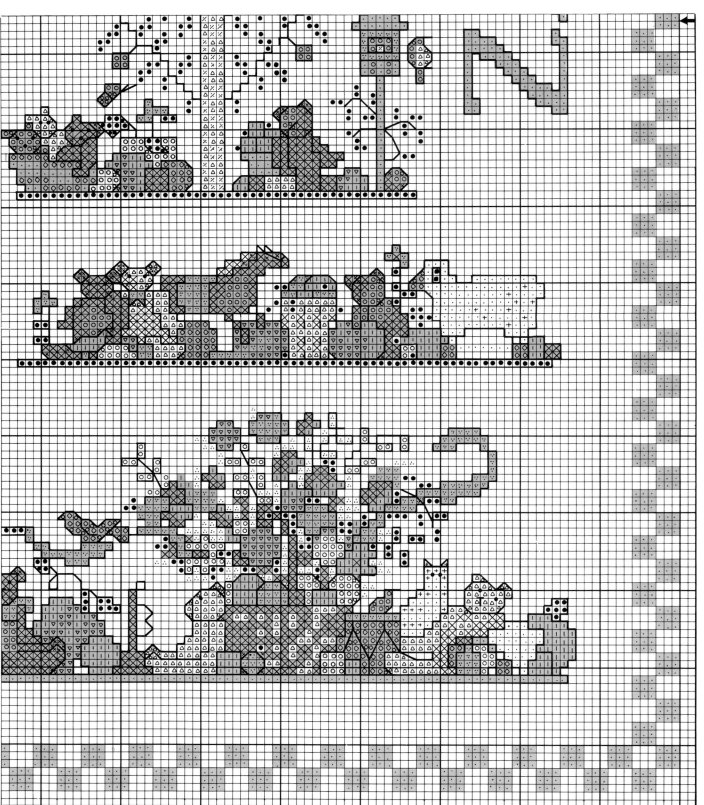

KITCHEN ANGEL

The designs are taken from **Bless This House**. Stitch the checkerboard border with Waste Canvas 18 over one thread. Cut the fabric 37″ × 7″ and the Waste Canvas 37″ × 3″. Repeat 35″ of checkerboard pattern for skirt bottom. The decorative border is the middle left design. Center and stitch two threads above the checkerboard border.

MATERIALS

1 yard of muslin (includes completed cross-stitch for apron and hat band); matching thread
⅛ yard of polyester fleece
Three small snap sets
Reynolds Saucy 100% cotton yarn (cream)
Large-eyed, sharp needle
10″ of ¼″-wide elastic
6″ of ⅛″-wide elastic
2-3 cups of sawdust

DIRECTIONS for body and wings

All seam allowances are ¼″.

1. Make patterns for head, body, arm, sleeve and wing transferring all information. Cut doll head, body, arm, sleeve and wing pieces from muslin according to patterns. Also cut two 4″ × 8″ pieces of muslin for a weight. Cut two wing pieces from fleece.

2. With right sides together, stitch two arm pieces, leaving an opening as indicated on pattern. Clip seam allowance at thumb. Turn. Stuff one arm firmly to within ½″ of top. Stitch the top edge. Repeat for second arm. Set aside.

3. Stitch a ⅛″-wide hem in the wrist edge of one sleeve. Stitch gathering threads in sleeve cap. With right sides together, stitch edges of sleeve piece together. Sew ⅛″-wide elastic ½″ above the hem, either by hand or with zigzag stitch over ⅛″-wide elastic. Gather to fit the wrist and secure. Stitch gathering threads in sleeve cap. Gather the sleeve to fit the arm. Pin together.

4. Stitch head piece to body piece at neck. Repeat.

5. Pin arms/sleeve piece to right side of one body piece with hands toward center of body; see pattern. With right sides of two body/head pieces together and with arms sandwiched between, stitch together.

6. To make weight, stitch together the two 4″ × 8″ pieces leaving a small opening. Turn. Fill with sawdust. Slipstitch the opening closed.

7. Turn seam allowance at bottom edge of body piece inside ¼″. Sew running stitch by hand around bottom edge. Stuff head and body firmly nearly to bottom edge. Insert weight. Pull threads to gather and secure.

8. Transfer hairline from pattern to doll head. Mark a light pencil line ¼″ in front of seam which joins two head pieces. Cut 24″ lengths of yarn. Double one 24″ strand and make one stitch on pencil line. Cut the yarn at the eye of the needle to release it. Then make additional stitches from 24″ lengths on pencil line close together. Pull hair to back of head and secure in "pony tail" with piece of yarn. Then, wrap hair toward head to make a doughnut-shaped bun. Secure bun with thread or glue. Again using two strands of yarn, make ½″-¾″ deep loops in a row for bangs on hairline. Continue to make second row of loops, tapering off toward ears. Add a third row at forehead, if desired.

9. To make wings, place two wing pieces with right sides together. Stitch short ends together. Then pin fleece to wrong side of one wing set. Stitch two wing sets with right sides together, leaving a small opening. Trim fleece from seam allowance. Turn. Slipstitch the opening closed. Topstitch around wings ⅛″ from edge. Then topstitch quilting lines as marked. Attach to back of body 1″ from neckline.

DIRECTIONS for hat, apron, skirt and collar

All seam allowances are ¼".

1. Make pattern for collar, transferring all information. Set aside. Trim apron piece to 35″ × 6″ with design centered and lower edge of checkerboard 1″ above bottom 35″ edge. Trim hat band to 8″ × 1½″ with top edge of checkerboard ⅜″ from top 8″ edge. From muslin cut the following pieces:

  One 7″–wide circle for hat
  One 1″ × 8″ strip for straps
  Two 2¼″ × 3¼″ pieces for bib
  46″ of 2″–wide strips for waistband/ties
  One 40″ × 7½″ piece for skirt
  1″ × 4″ bias for collar
  Collar pieces according to pattern

2. To make hat, stitch ends of hat band together. Then fold hat band with wrong sides together to measure 8″ × ¾″. Stitch gathering threads around outside edge of circle piece and gather to fit hat band. With design side of hat band and right side of circle piece together, match and stitch around top edges. Zigzag all raw edges. Turn.

3. To make apron, hem sides and bottom edges of design piece. Mark center of apron skirt on waist edge and stitch gathering threads on the raw edge. Gather the skirt to 9½″.

4. Piece together 2″–wide strips for waistband/ties to make one 16″ strip. Fold strip to measure 1″ × 46″. Mark center on long edge of waistband/ties strip. Match the centers of apron and waistband; stitch together. Turn long edge of waistband/ties under hiding all raw edges. Topstitch the lower, long edge. Turn ends under to form diagonals and stitch closed.

5. Fold the piece for straps with right sides together to measure ½″ × 8″. Stitch the long edge and one end. Trim to ⅛″ seam allowance. Turn. Cut into two 4″ straps.

6. With right sides of bib pieces together, sandwich the strap pieces on each side of the top edge matching the raw ends of straps with one raw edge of bib. Stitch across top and side edges. Zigzag the raw edge. Turn. Mark the bib center.

7. Match centers of bib and waistband placing the bib behind. Topstitch the folded long edge of waistband securing bib in stitching.

8. Sew snap sets to ends of straps and waistband where sides of apron skirt end.

9. To make skirt, fold the 7½″ ends together and stitch (this is the center back seam). Fold bottom edge under ½″ double and hem. Fold top edge over ½″ to the wrong side at the waist. Turn under the raw edge and stitch to make casing for elastic leaving an opening. Thread the elastic through the casing. Overlap the ends ½″ and secure. Slipstitch the casing closed.

10. To make collar, place two collar pieces right sides together. Stitch the curved edge. Turn. Repeat for remaining pieces. With bias strip and both collar pieces right sides together, stitch the long edge with collar pieces touching in center. Trim the seam allowance to ⅛″. Fold bias over and slipstitch the edge. Turn ends under and stitch. Sew snap set to ends.

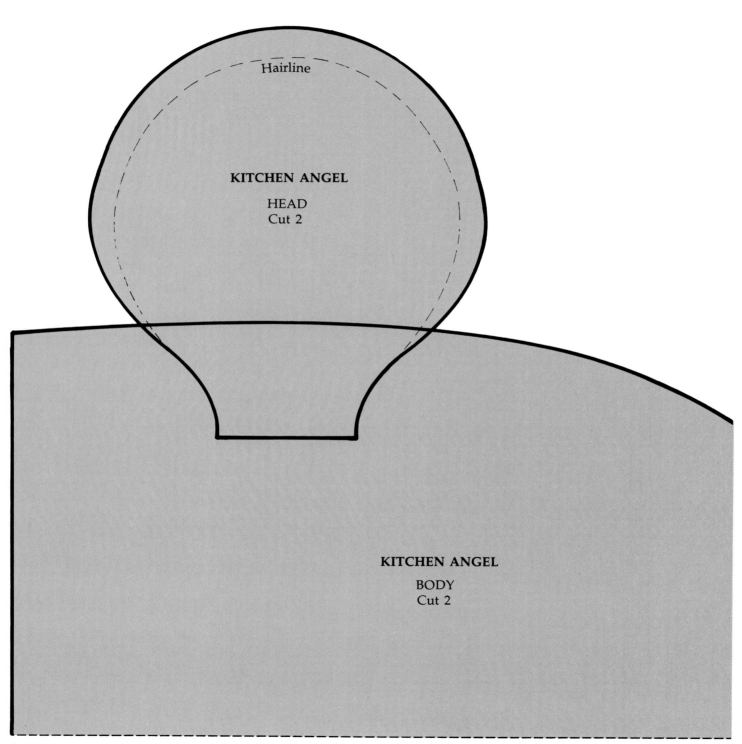

Hairline

KITCHEN ANGEL

HEAD
Cut 2

KITCHEN ANGEL

BODY
Cut 2

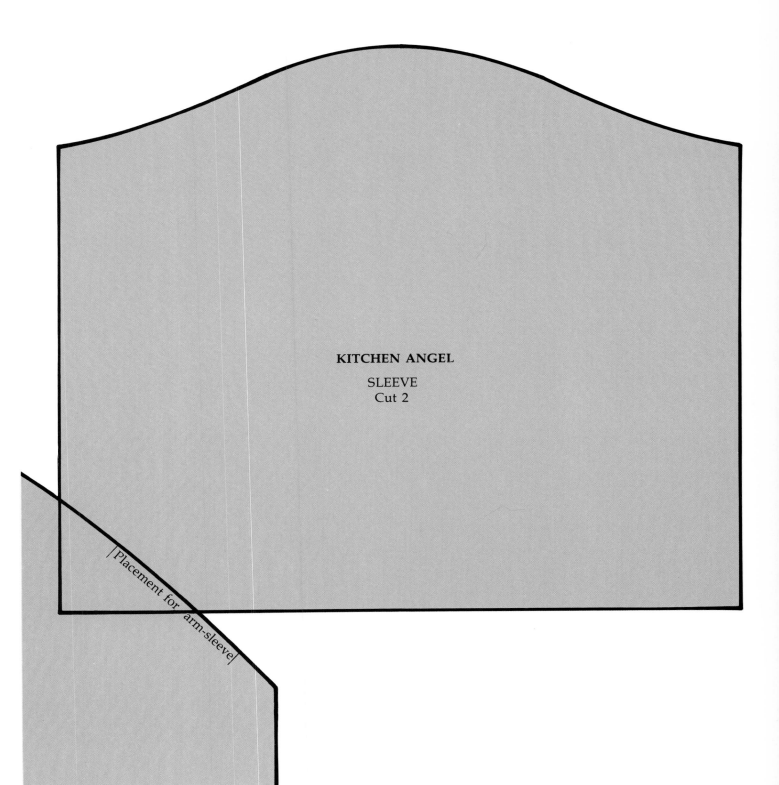

KITCHEN ANGEL

SLEEVE
Cut 2

Placement for arm-sleeve

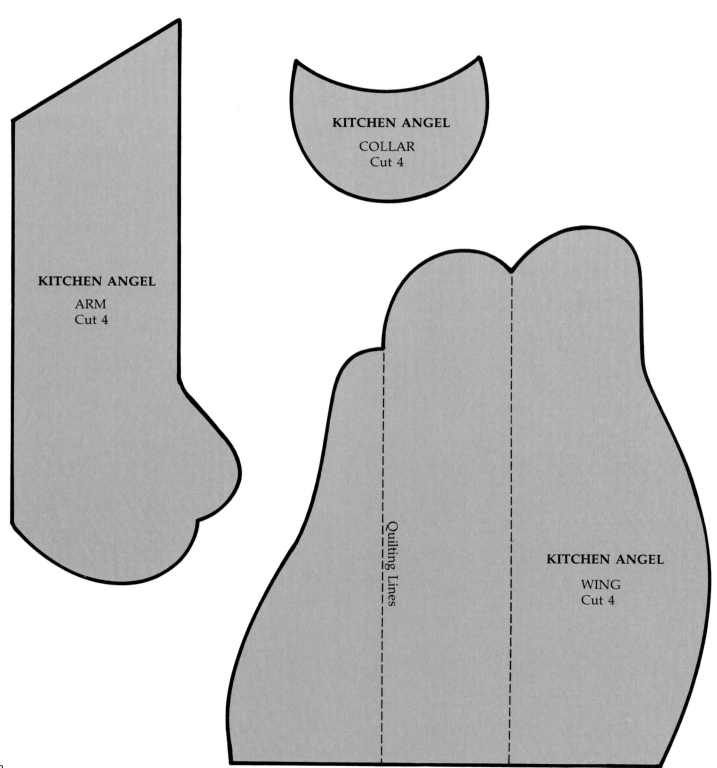

KITCHEN ANGEL

COLLAR
Cut 4

KITCHEN ANGEL

ARM
Cut 4

Quilting Lines

KITCHEN ANGEL

WING
Cut 4

LITTLE TOY BORDER

The row of toys is from the bottom border of **Bless This House**. Stitched on ivory Belfast Linen 32 over two threads, the finished design size is 9⅞" × ¾". The fabric was cut 16" × 7". Center the design with bottom edge of design 3¾" from bottom edge of fabric. The stitch count is 158 × 13.

MATERIALS

Completed cross-stitch on ivory Belfast Linen 32; matching thread
Five diamond-shaped red wood buttons; matching thread
⅝ yard of ⅛"–wide blue satin ribbon; matching thread

DIRECTIONS

1. Stitch a ¼"–deep tuck ½" below and parallel to the bottom edge of the design. Press the tuck down.

2. Slipstitch ribbon 1¼" below and parallel to the stitching line of the tuck.

3. Mark placement for five buttons 2¼" apart, beginning in the center. Sew the buttons over the ribbon.

FOOTSTOOL FOR HOME

The houses were taken from **Bless This House**. Stitch two houses 2" apart on amaretto Murano 30 over two threads. The finished design size is 17⅞" × 9". The fabric was cut 22" × 18". The stitch count is 269 × 135. Insert in footstool following manufacturer's instructions.

Patchwork quilts are
memories pieced together
and stitched with the
threads of tradition.
Swatches of grandma's
apron rekindle wonderful
scents from her kitchen and
scraps of an uncle's tie
recall stories told while
sitting on his lap.

THE COMFORTER

Stitched on cream Belfast Linen 32 over two threads, the finished design size is 15⅝" × 12¼". The fabric was cut 22" × 19".

FABRIC	DESIGN SIZES
Aida 11	22¾" × 17⅞"
Aida 14	17⅞" × 14"
Aida 18	13⅞" × 10⅞"
Hardanger 22	11⅜" × 8⅞"

Step One: Cross-stitch (two strands)

ANCHOR   DMC (used for sample)

1	White
1	White (one strand)
926	Ecru
886	677 Old Gold-vy. lt.
886	677 Old Gold-vy. lt. (one strand)
891	676 Old Gold-lt.
891	676 Old Gold-lt. (one strand)
324	922 Copper-lt.
349	921 Copper
339	920 Copper-med.
339	920 Copper-med. (one strand)
341	919 Red Copper
4146	754 Peach Flesh-lt.
9	760 Salmon
9	760 Salmon (one strand)
11	3328 Salmon-med.
13	347 Salmon-dk.
22	816 Garnet
871	3041 Antique Violet-med.
871	3041 Antique Violet-med. (one strand)
900	928 Slate Green-lt.
900	928 Slate Green-lt. (one strand)
920	932 Antique Blue-lt.
920	932 Antique Blue-lt. (one strand)

921	931 Antique Blue-med.
921	931 Antique Blue-med. (one strand)
922	930 Antique Blue-dk.
922	930 Antique Blue-dk. (one strand)
843	3364 Pine Green
843	3364 Pine Green (one strand)
216	367 Pistachio Green-dk.
216	367 Pistachio Green-dk. (one strand)
309	435 Brown-vy. lt.
371	433 Brown-med.

Step Two: Backstitch (one strand)

216	367 Pistachio Green-dk. (flower stems)
371	433 Brown-med. (tree branches)
401	844 Beaver Gray-ultra dk. (all else)

Step Three: French Knots (one strand)

401	844 Beaver Gray-ultra dk.

62

Stitch Count: 250 × 196

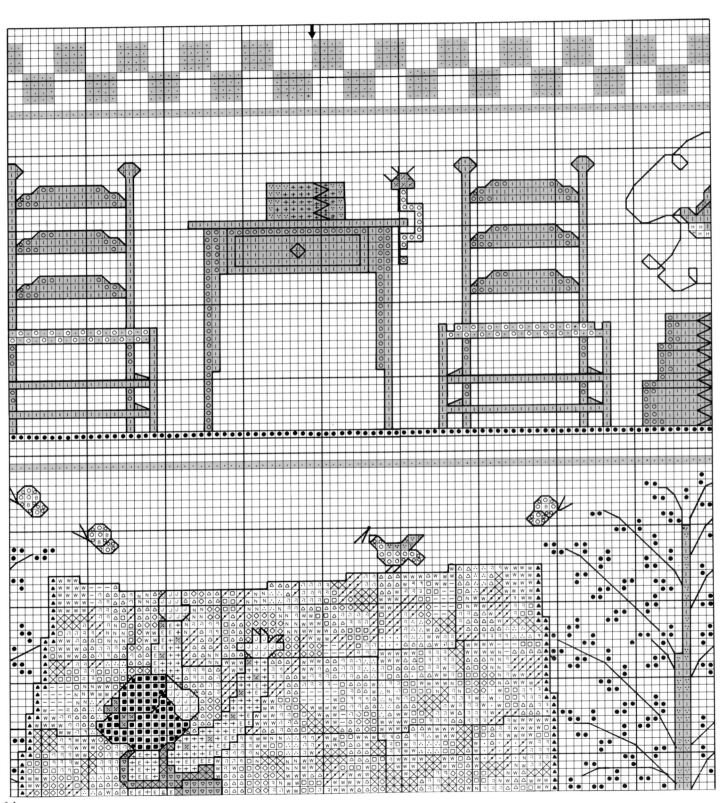

NOW MAY OUR LORD WHO LOVED US

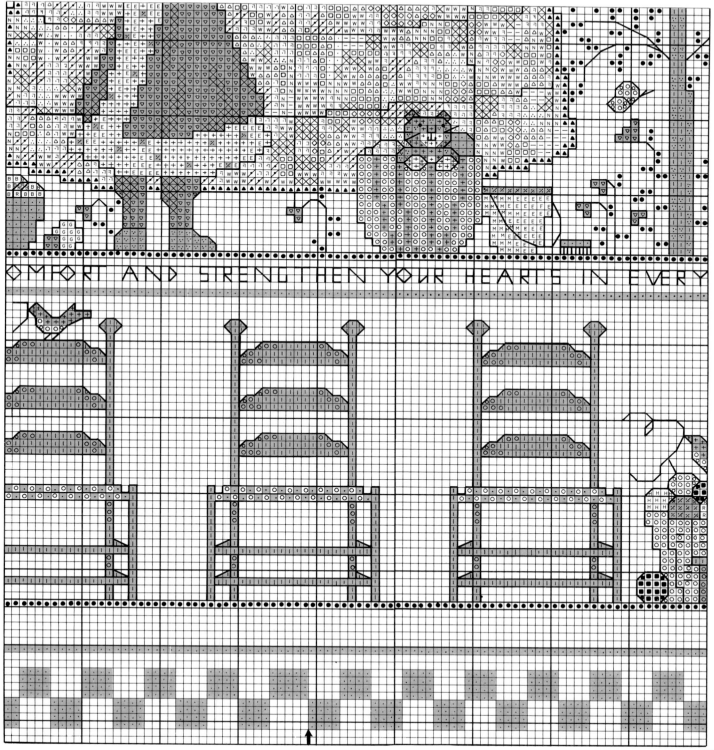

POTPOURRI BOXES

The motifs are taken from each corner of **The Comforter**. Stitched on cream Hardanger 22 over one thread, the finished design size for each is 4⅛" × 4⅛". The fabric was cut 6" × 6" and the stitch count is 46 × 46 for each.

MATERIALS for one
Completed cross-stitch on cream Hardanger 22
24" of small molding*
24" of 1"–wide molding*
Two 5" × 5" pieces of glass
Clear silicone caulking
3" piece of ribbon
One 7" × 7" piece of dark colored mat board
Glue

DIRECTIONS

1. Trim design pieces three threads outside stitching. Remove one thread from all edges.

2. Construct frame from small molding to hold a 5" × 5" piece of glass.

3. Place design piece between two layers of glass, positioned as desired. Seal glass in frame with clear silicone caulking.

4. Miter large molding making the front face of the molding the side of the box. This will make the rabbet the top of the box so the design piece frame will fit into the recess (Diagram 1). Construct the frame to measure slightly larger than the outside edges of the small molding. Touch up stain on inside surfaces of molding, if needed. Cut dark mat board to fit bottom of larger molding. Glue to molding to make bottom of box.

5. Fold ribbon in half to make 1½" loop. Glue ends to center of lower edge of small frame.

* Molding is measured along the rabbet (the lip or recess) where the framed item and glass rest. Additional molding is needed for mitering the corners. Buy enough small molding for a 5" × 5" piece of glass. Measure the outside edge of the small molding, adding enough for the mitered corners, to determine the length needed for the larger molding.

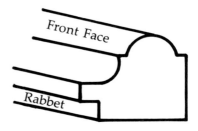

A. Standard placement for molding.

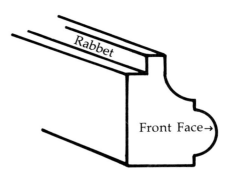

B. Placement for molding for potpourri box.

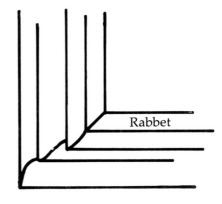

C. Mitered corner for potpourri box.

HANGING OUT THE QUILT

The design is the center block on **The Comforter**. Stitched on daffodil damask Aida 14 over one thread, the finished design size is 9⅝″ × 5⅞″. The fabric was cut 16″ × 12″. The stitch count is 134 × 83.

The mat and frame for this picture are both covered with wallpaper. Select a wallpaper border. Then have a mat cut which is wide enough for the border. Miter the corners and attach the border to the mat with spray adhesive.

Select molding with a simple pattern. For the frame, measure the outside edge of the mat adding extra for the mitered corners. Cut a single strip of wallpaper longer and wider than the molding, allowing for all edges to be covered. Cover the wrong side of the wallpaper and the right side of the molding with spray adhesive. Place the two together, working out air bubbles as you go. Then cut and construct the frame.

ALICE IN WONDERLAND

Whether having tea with the Mad Hatter or playing croquet with the Queen, Alice is ready for any important date in her royal blue dress and pinafore cross-stitched with a cute and cuddly kitten. See instructions on page 136.

Freedom is an inherent part of our country's heritage. We celebrate it not only on Independence Day but in every creative expression as well. Hoorah for another year of liberty!

THE LIBERTY

Stitched on cream Belfast Linen 32 over two threads, the finished design size is 14¾″ × 11¾″. The fabric was cut 21″ × 18″.

FABRIC	DESIGN SIZES
Aida 11	21½″ × 17⅛″
Aida 14	16⅞″ × 13½″
Aida 18	13⅛″ × 10½″
Hardanger 22	10¾″ × 8⅝″

Step One: Cross-stitch (two strands)

ANCHOR   **DMC** (used for sample)

ANCHOR		DMC	
926	=		Ecru
891	·	676	Old Gold-lt.
901		680	Old Gold-dk.
778	·	948	Peach Flesh-vy. lt.
9	○	760	Salmon
11	✕	3328	Salmon-med.
19	▽	817	Coral Red-vy. dk.
22		816	Garnet
168	■	597	Turquoise
920	∴	932	Antique Blue-lt.
921	▲	931	Antique Blue-med.
922	✕	930	Antique Blue-dk.
851	●	924	Slate Green-vy. dk.
216	+	367	Pistachio Green-dk.
885	○	739	Tan-ultra vy. lt.
307	▢	977	Golden Brown-lt.
339	△	920	Copper-med.
341		919	Red Copper

Step Two: Backstitch (one strand)

851		924 Slate Green-vy. dk. (alphabet)
341		919 Red Copper (tree branches)
401		844 Beaver Gray-ultra dk. (all else except balloon strings and inside drum)

Step Three: Long Loose Stitch (one strand)

401		844 Beaver Gray-ultra dk. (balloon strings, inside drum)

Step Four: French Knots (one strand)

401		844 Beaver Gray-ultra dk. (bird's eye)

Now the Lord is the spirit:
where the spirit of the
Lord is, there is liberty
2 Corinthians 3:17

Stitch Count: 237 × 189

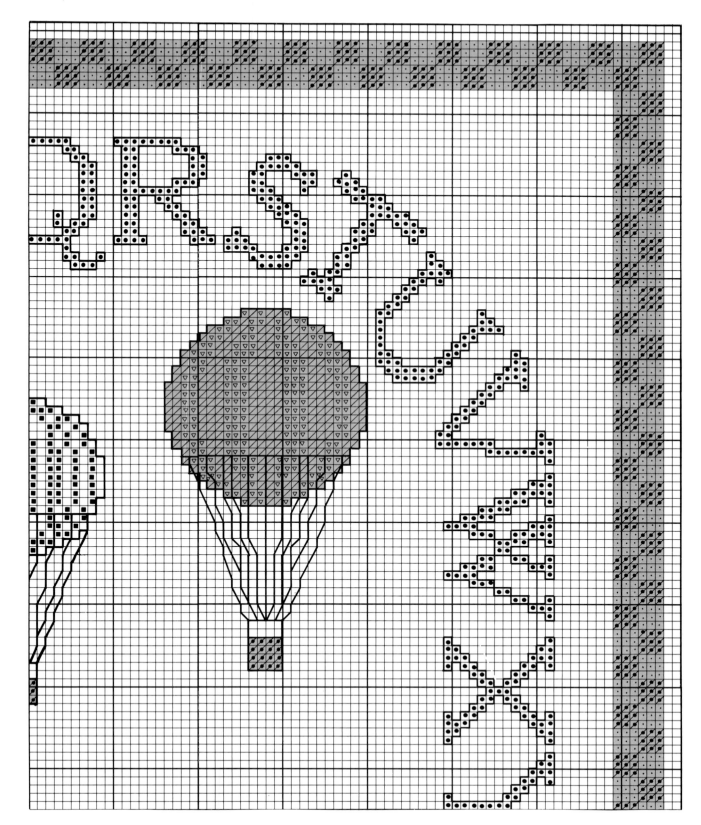

CHECKERBOARD PILLOW

Stitch on ivory damask Aida 14 over one thread with design centered; see photo. The finished design size is 9¾" × 10⅜" and the fabric was cut 15" × 15".

MATERIALS
Completed cross-stitch on ivory damask Aida 14; matching thread
1 yard of yellow fabric
1 yard of ivory fabric
4 yards of medium cording
Stuffing

DIRECTIONS
All seam allowances are ¼"

1. Cut the design piece 14" × 12½" with the design centered. From the yellow fabric, cut three 2"–wide strips to equal at least 34½" each. From the ivory fabric, cut a 23" × 21½" piece for the pillow back and three 2"–wide strips to equal at least 34½" each. Also from the ivory fabric, cut a 1½"–wide bias, piecing as needed to equal 4 yards. Make 4 yards of corded piping.

2. With right sides together, stitch two yellow strips with a ivory strip between. Cut into twenty-three 2"–wide segments (Diagram 1). Then, with right sides together, stitch two ivory strips with a yellow strip between. Cut into twenty-three 2"–wide segments.

3. Piece together fifteen checkerboard segments to make borders for top and bottom of pillow (Diagram 2), noting the color pattern of the bottom is opposite the top. Piece two identical border pieces for the sides using eight checkerboard segments for each side.

4. Cut a 53" length of piping. Stitch the piping to the right side of the design piece keeping the corners square.

5. Stitch the side borders to the design piece with right sides together, stitching on stitching line of piping. Repeat with top and bottom borders (Diagram 3). Adjust checkerboard seams if necessary to fit the design piece size.

6. With remaining piping, stitch to the outside edge of the border keeping the corners square.

7. Pin the front and the back of the pillow with right sides together. Stitch on stitching line of piping, keeping the corners square and leaving a 6" opening in one edge. Trim corners. Turn.

8. Stitch in-the-ditch of the piping on the inside of the border and through both layers, leaving a small opening adjacent to the outside opening. Stuff the pillow firmly by reaching through both openings. Close the inside opening by hand or machine. Slip-stitch the outside opening closed.

DIAGRAM 1

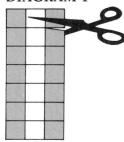

DIAGRAM 2

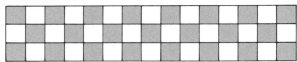

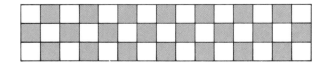

DIAGRAM 3

HANGING SACHETS

The designs were taken from **The Liberty**; see photo. The man with balloons was stitched on pewter Murano 30; the man and woman were stitched on ash rose Murano 30; the woman with a flag was stitched on cracked wheat Murano 30. All designs were stitched over two threads. The fabric was cut 6″ × 8″ for each motif.

MATERIALS for one
Completed cross-stitch
4½″ × 6″ piece of matching fabric for back
1½ yards burgundy/mauve/peach braided trim
Stuffing
Potpourri

DIRECTIONS

All seam allowances are ¼″.

1. Trim design piece to 4″ × 5¾″ with design centered and bottom of design ⅝″ from bottom edge. Cut one 4″ × 5¾″ piece for back.

2. Stitch front to back with right sides together, leaving a small opening. Clip corners. Turn. Stuff moderately. Fill with potpourri. Slipstitch the opening closed.

3. Finish with one tassel at center bottom or two tassels at bottom corners.

For one tassel, cut one 29″ piece of braid. With ends of trim together, measure 4″ from ends and wrap tightly with one strand from trim. With tassel at center bottom, slipstitch trim to bottom and sides of sachet over seam. Fray free ends.

For two tassels, cut one 11″ piece and one 32″ piece of braided trim. Slipstitch center of trim over bottom seam leaving ends of trim free. Place 32″ piece of trim at sides and over top of sachet. Wrap bottom trim and side trim together, wrap tightly at corners with one strand from trim. Fray free ends.

LITTLE MISS MUFFET

Little Miss Muffet will be sitting pretty in this turquoise and white dress—until the spider scares her away. Instructions for her dress begin on page 138.

A walk through the park reveals an oasis filled with the beauties of nature and the quiet rhythm of life - simple pleasures indeed.

GARDEN IN THE PARK

Stitched on ivory damask Aida 14 over one thread, the finished design size is 16⅞" × 13½". The fabric was cut 23" × 20".

FABRIC	DESIGN SIZES
Aida 11	21½" × 17⅛"
Aida 18	13⅛" × 10½"
Hardanger 22	10¾" × 8⅝"

Step One: Cross-stitch (two strands)

ANCHOR   **DMC** (used for sample)

886		677 Old Gold-vy. lt.
891		676 Old Gold-lt.
324		721 Orange Spice-med.
326		922 Copper-lt.
349		921 Copper
339		920 Copper-med.
4146		754 Peach Flesh-lt.
11		3328 Salmon-med.
13		347 Salmon-dk.
19		817 Coral Red-vy. dk.
869		3042 Antique Violet-lt.
871		3041 Antique Violet-med.
920		932 Antique Blue-lt.
921		931 Antique Blue-med.
851		924 Slate Green-vy. dk.
843		3364 Pine Green
216		367 Pistachio Green-dk.
246		319 Pistachio Green-vy. dk.
878		501 Blue Green-dk.
900		3024 Brown Gray-vy. lt.
8581		3023 Brown Gray-lt.

Step Two: Backstitch (one strand)

851		924 Slate Green-vy. dk. (alphabet)
246		319 Pistachio Green-vy. dk. (vines between leaves)
401		844 Beaver Gray-ultra dk. (all else)

Step Three: French Knots (one strand)

401		844 Beaver Gray-ultra dk.

Step Four: Smyrna Cross (one strand)

921		931 Antique Blue-med.

Stitch Count: 237 × 189

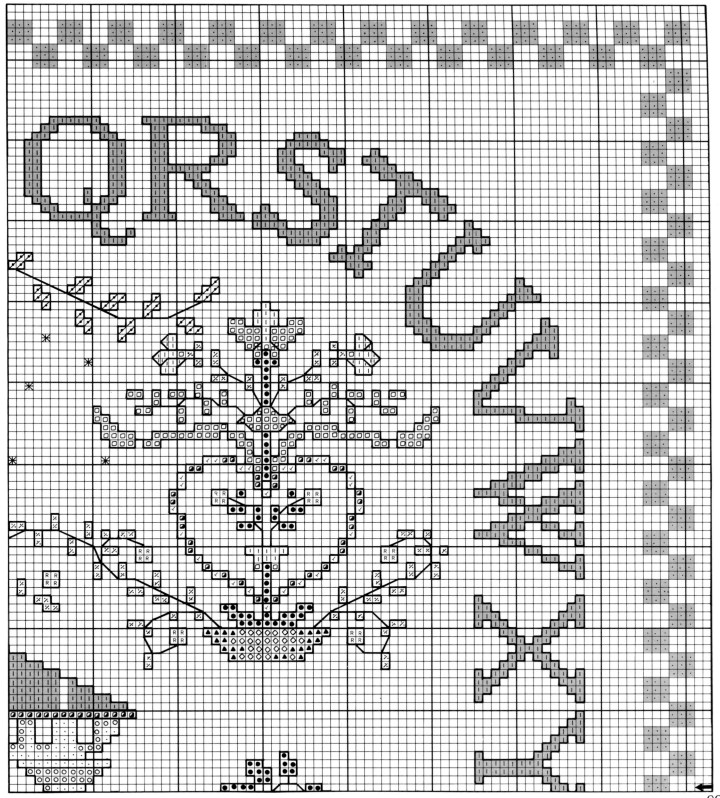

92

GARDENER'S ENSEMBLE

The designs were taken from **Garden in the Park**. The heart design was stitched on pink Dublin Linen 25 over two threads. The towel design was stitched on country Aida 14 over one thread. The finished design size for the heart is 2⅝" × 3¼"; the towel is 9⅛" × 2⅜". The fabric was cut 7" × 7" for the heart and 16" × 23" for the towel. The stitch count is 33 × 41 for the heart and 127 × 34 for the towel.

MATERIALS for one towel
Completed cross-stitch on country Aida 14; matching thread
14½" of antique crochet trim

DIRECTIONS
1. Trim design piece to 22" × 14½" with design centered 1½" from bottom edge. Hem all edges of design piece.

2. Attach crochet trim to one end.

MATERIALS for one heart
⅛ yard of pink Dublin Linen 25 (includes completed cross-stitch design); matching thread
Stuffing
⅝ yard of white twisted cording

DIRECTIONS

All seam allowances are ¼".

1. Make pattern. Place pattern over design piece with design centered and bottom edge of basket 1¼" from bottom center point of heart. Cut out. Then cut one heart from unstitched linen for back.

2. With right sides together, stitch around edges leaving a small opening. Clip seam allowance at top center. Turn. Stuff firmly. Slipstitch the opening closed.

3. Slipstitch cording to outside edge of heart beginning at top center point of heart and leaving a 6" tail at beginning end to make loop. When stitching is complete, twist cord once. Tuck under last stitches and tack at center back.

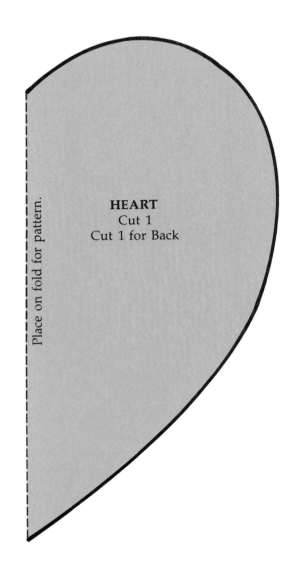

Place on fold for pattern.

HEART
Cut 1
Cut 1 for Back

BUTTONS AND BORDER

The border is the bottom border motif on **Garden in the Park**. Stitched on ivory Belfast Linen 32 over two threads, the finished design size is 9⅞" × ¾". The fabric was cut 16" × 7". The stitch count is 158 × 13.

MATERIALS

Completed cross-stitch on cream Belfast Linen 32; matching thread
½ yard of ⅛"–wide red satin ribbon; matching thread
Three ½"–wide green/cream buttons; matching thread
Two ½"–wide red/cream buttons; matching thread

DIRECTIONS

1. Complete Step 1 from **Little Toy Border** on page 59. Complete Step 2, placing ribbon 1" from stitching line. Complete Step 3, placing buttons 2" apart.

EYEGLASS CASE AND MAKEUP POUCH

The basket/bouquet design came from the left bottom corner of **Garden in the Park**. Stitched on daffodil damask Aida 14 over one thread, the finished design size is 2⅝" × 2⅞". The fabric was cut 6" × 9" for the case and 9" × 8" for the pouch. The stitch count is 37 × 41.

MATERIALS for eyeglass case

Completed cross-stitch on daffodil damask Aida 14; matching thread
One 5½″ × 9″ piece of unstitched daffodil damask Aida 14 for back
¼ yard of light yellow fabric for lining; matching thread
¼ yard of gray satin
¾ yard of small cording
One set of 4″–wide hardware
Tracing paper for pattern

DIRECTIONS

All seam allowances are ¼″.

1. Make pattern. Place pattern over design piece with center of design 4½″ from top edge. Cut out. Also cut one piece like pattern from unstitched Aida. From fabric for lining, cut two pieces like pattern and two 1″ × 4½″ pieces for casing. Cut 1″-wide bias from gray satin, piecing as needed, to equal 27″. Make 27″ of corded piping.

2. To make casing for hardware, match top edge of casing piece to top edge of lining on wrong side. Stitch both edges of casing. Insert hardware. Repeat for other lining piece. Set aside.

3. Cut two 4½″ pieces of piping. With right sides together, stitch one piece to the top edge of each piece of Aida. Then stitch one lining piece to one Aida piece, right sides together, on stitching line of piping only. Repeat.

4. Place Aida/lining design piece with right sides up. Stitch remaining piping to one side edge beginning with 1″ of piping above Aida on lining. Stitch around sides and bottom of Aida, ending with 1″ on second edge of lining.

5. With right sides of both Aida/lining pieces together, match and stitch around sides and ends on stitching line of piping leaving a small opening in lining. Turn. Slipstitch the opening closed. Tuck lining inside.

MATERIALS for makeup pouch

Completed cross-stitch on daffodil damask Aida 14; matching thread
One 6½″ × 7½″ piece of unstitched daffodil damask Aida 14 for back
¼ yard of light yellow fabric for lining; matching thread
¼ yard of gray satin
¾ yard of small cording
One set of 4″–wide hardware
Tracing paper for pattern

DIRECTIONS

All seam allowances are ¼″.

1. Make pattern. Place pattern over design piece with center of design 3½″ from top edge. Cut out. Also cut one piece like pattern from unstitched Aida. From fabric for lining, cut two pieces like pattern and two 1″ × 4½″ pieces for casing. Cut 1″-wide bias from gray satin, piecing as needed, to equal 27″. Make 27″ of corded piping.

2. To make casing for hardware, match top edge of casing piece to top edge of lining on wrong side. Stitch both edges of casing. Insert hardware. Repeat for other lining piece. Set aside.

3. Cut two 5″ pieces of piping. With right sides together, stitch one piece to the top edge of each piece of Aida. Then stitch one lining piece to one Aida piece, right sides together, on stitching line of piping only. Repeat.

4. Complete Steps 4 and 5 of eyeglass case directions.

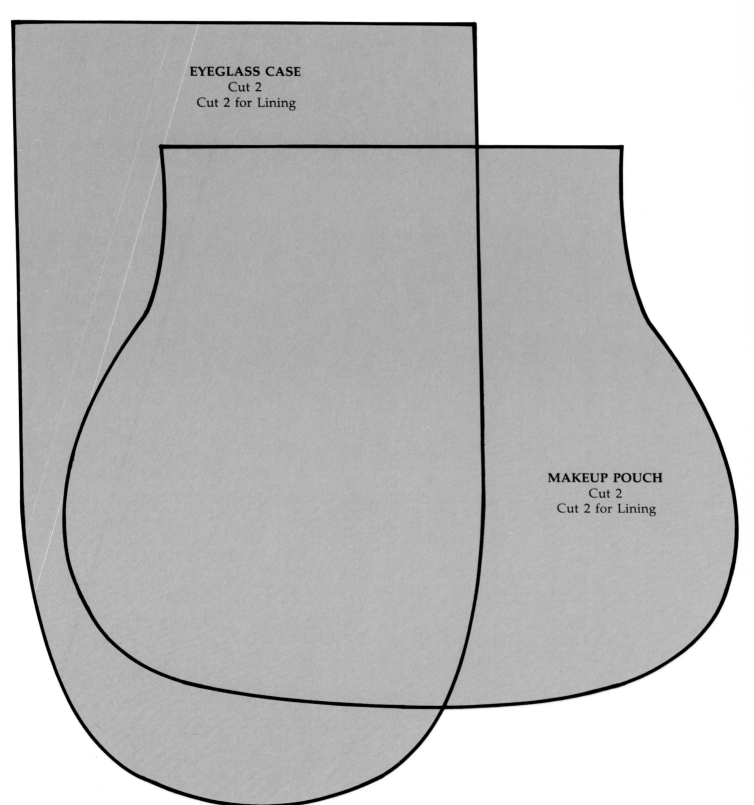

EYEGLASS CASE
Cut 2
Cut 2 for Lining

MAKEUP POUCH
Cut 2
Cut 2 for Lining

Ellen Stouffer sends good
tidings with a festive
holiday painting.
Reminiscent of the sights
and sounds of Christmas,
this sampler reveals the
magic of the season.

A VERY MERRY CHRISTMAS

Stitched on ivory damask Aida 14 over one thread, the finished design size is 17½″ × 13⅞″. The fabric was cut 24″ × 20″.

FABRIC	DESIGN SIZES
Aida 11	22¼″ × 17¾″
Aida 18	13⅝″ × 10⅞″
Hardanger 22	11⅛″ × 8⅞″

Step One: Cross-stitch (two strands)

ANCHOR		DMC (used for sample)	
926			Ecru
306	N	725	Topaz
886	I	677	Old Gold-vy. lt.
891	•	676	Old Gold-lt.
890	O	729	Old Gold-med.
323	E	722	Orange Spice-lt.
324	H	721	Orange Spice-med.
349	–	922	Copper-lt.
339	O	920	Copper-med.
4146	%	754	Peach Flesh-lt.
9	□	760	Salmon
13	X	347	Salmon-dk.
869	S	3042	Antique Violet-lt.
871	B	3041	Antique Violet-med.
900	I	928	Slate Green-lt.
920	▽	932	Antique Blue-lt.
921	∴	931	Antique Blue-med.
922	▲	930	Antique Blue-dk.
843	∴	3364	Pine Green
215	△	320	Pistachio Green-med.
246	■	319	Pistachio Green-vy. dk.
378	⌐	841	Beige Brown-lt.
380	◢	839	Beige Brown-dk.
900	◇	648	Beaver Gray-lt.
8581	X	647	Beaver Gray-med.
401	●	844	Beaver Gray-ultra dk.

Step Two: Backstitch (one strand)

13		347 Salmon-dk. (candy canes)
246		319 Pistachio Green-vy. dk. (stems, vines)
401		844 Beaver Gray-ultra dk. (all else)

Step Three: French Knots (one strand)

13	◆	347 Salmon-dk.
401	●	844 Beaver Gray-ultra dk.

Stitch Count: 245 × 195

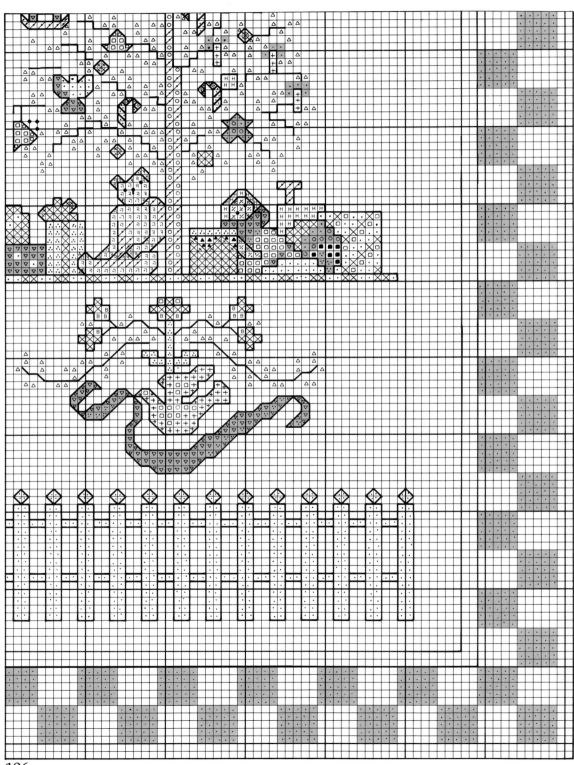

COLLECTOR'S PILLOW

Stitched on sand Dublin 25 over two threads, the finished design size is 7¼″ × 8⅜″. The fabric was cut 10″ × 15″. Also needed: approximately fifty miniature assorted ornaments.

Step One: Cross-stitch (two strands)

ANCHOR		DMC (used for sample)
891	○	676 Old Gold-lt.
11	=	3328 Salmon-med.
187	⊠	992 Aquamarine
216	▫	367 Pistachio Green-dk.
378	U	841 Beige Brown-lt.
380	▲	839 Beige Brown-dk.

Step Two: Backstitch (one strand)

216	367 Pistachio Green-dk. (tree)
401	844 Beaver Gray-ultra dk. (all else)

Step Three: Beadwork

Blue
Red (strings, in and out points)

Step Four: Ornaments (place on tree as desired)

MATERIALS

Completed cross-stitch on sand Dublin 25; matching thread
½ yard of burgundy print fabric*; matching thread
¼ yard of dark green print fabric; matching thread
One 8½″ × 12½″ piece of flannel
Scraps of two coordinating print fabrics
Fifty miniature assorted ornaments (including twenty icicles and seven candy canes)
One tube of red beads
One 1 ¾″ sled ornament
Stuffing
Embroidery floss: burgundy and gold
One 8½″ × 12½″ piece of tan fabric
Small pieces of ¼″ foam for packages

DIRECTIONS

All seam allowances are ¼″.

1. Trim design piece to 8½″ × 12½″ with design centered horizontally and 2½″ from the top edge. Pin flannel to wrong side of design piece. Stitch side edges only of tan piece and design piece with right sides together. Trim flannel from seam allowance. Turn. Press edges. Set aside.

2. Cut two 12½″ × 17″ pieces from burgundy print fabric*. Cut four 1¾″ × 25″ pieces of dark green print fabric.

3. Fold one green strip to measure ⅞″ wide. Stitch long edge. Turn. Press with seam in center of back. Repeat.

4. Stitch one green strip to pillow front with inside edge 4″ from and parallel to the vertical center. Leave all extra length on the bottom edge; stop stitching and backstitch ½″ from bottom edge. Repeat with second strip on pillow front and remaining two on pillow back.

5. Decorate design piece using floss which matches the tree to attach items. String the beads and attach first. Then add remaining items. To make packages, cut four pieces of foam in the following sizes: 1″ × 1¼″, ¾″ × 1½″, ¾″ × ¾″ and ½″ × ½″. "Wrap" with fabric scraps and slipstitch to secure. Tie with six-strand lengths of floss. Tack to design piece.

6. Pin design piece to pillow front between green strips. Pin ends of strips to pillow front and back pieces to keep out of seams. Stitch pillow front and back together, leaving an opening in one end. Clip corners. Turn. Stuff firmly. Slipstitch the opening closed.

7. Tack sled among packages. Tie strips into bows at bottom of pillow. Knot ends.

* Note: The wrong side of the fabric will serve as the right side.

Stitch Count: 91 × 104

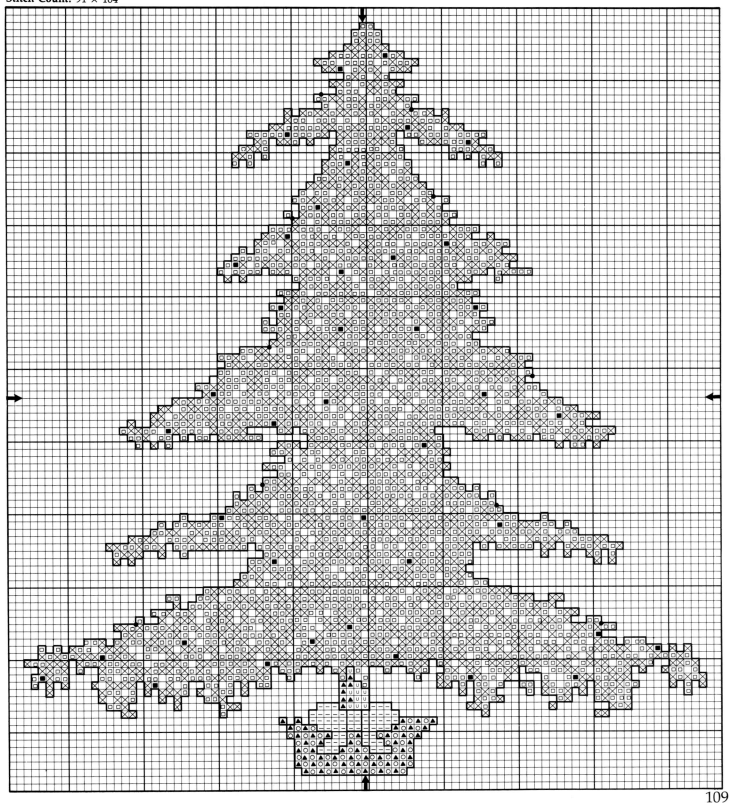

A CHRISTMAS WELCOME

Stitched on driftwood Belfast Linen 32 over two threads, the finished design size is 9⅝″ × 9½″. The fabric was cut 14″ × 14″.

Step One: Cross-stitch (two strands)

ANCHOR			DMC	(used for sample)
306	B	B	725	Topaz
323	H	A	722	Orange Spice-lt.
349	◇	A	921	Copper
341	●	A	919	Red Copper
8	∴	A	761	Salmon-lt.
9	+	◢	760	Salmon
11	·	◢	3328	Salmon-med.
13	△	◢	347	Salmon-dk.
101	G		327	Antique Violet-dk.
168	O	◢	597	Turquoise
920	%	◢	932	Antique Blue-lt.
921	✕	◢	931	Antique Blue-med.
779	◢	◢	926	Slate Green-dk.
851	■		924	Slate Green-vy. dk.
843	N		3364	Pine Green
216	◆		367	Pistachio Green-dk.
373	=	◢	422	Hazel Nut Brown-lt.
309	▢		435	Brown-vy. lt.
371	▲		433	Brown-med.

Step Two: Backstitch (one strand)

216		367 Pistachio Green-dk. (flower stems)
401		844 Beaver Gray-ultra dk. (all else)

Step Three: French Knots (one strand)

401	●	844 Beaver Gray-ultra dk.

MATERIALS

1¼ yards of driftwood Belfast Linen 32 (includes completed cross-stitch design); matching thread
1¼ yards of small cording
Stuffing
Paper for pattern

DIRECTIONS

All seam allowances are ¼″.

1. Make pattern for wreath by drawing a circle 11¾″ wide. Draw a second circle 2¾″ wide in the center.

2. Center pattern over design piece and cut. From linen, cut one piece like pattern for back and 1″–wide bias piecing as needed to equal 45½″. Make 45½″ of corded piping.

3. Stitch piping around inside and outside edges on right side of design piece. With right sides of design piece and back together, stitch on stitching line of piping around the outside edge. Turn. Slipstitch a small distance of inside edge and stuff that area moderately. Continue to slipstitch and stuff moderately around entire inside circle.

...and the life was the light of men

Stitch Count: 154 × 152

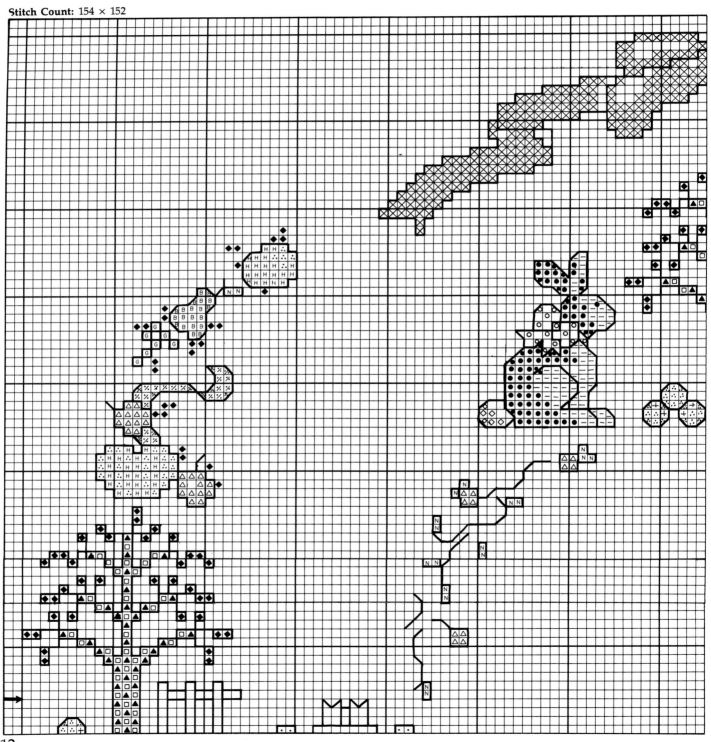

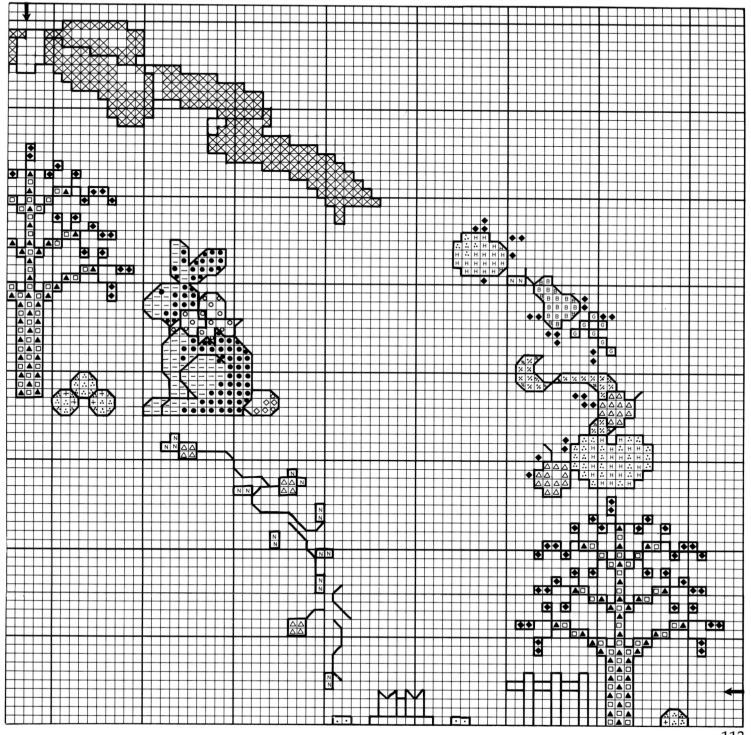

A TRIO OF STOCKINGS

All stocking designs were stitched on yellow Dublin Linen 25 over two threads. The finished design size for the ship is 5″ × 3¼″ and the rocking horse is 4⅞″ × 5⅛″. The fabric was cut 10″ × 13″ for the small ruffle band and maroon band stocking and 8″ × 5½″ for the large blue band stocking.

Step One: Cross-stitch (two strands)

ANCHOR   DMC (used for sample)

886		677 Old Gold-vy. lt.
891		676 Old Gold-lt.
890		729 Old Gold-med.
323		721 Orange Spice-med.
326		720 Orange Spice-dk.
324		922 Copper-lt.
339		920 Copper-med.
9		760 Salmon
11		3328 Salmon-med.
13		347 Salmon-dk.

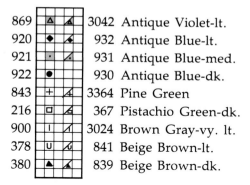

869		3042 Antique Violet-lt.
920		932 Antique Blue-lt.
921		931 Antique Blue-med.
922		930 Antique Blue-dk.
843		3364 Pine Green
216		367 Pistachio Green-dk.
900		3024 Brown Gray-vy. lt.
378		841 Beige Brown-lt.
380		839 Beige Brown-dk.

Step Two: Backstitch (one strand)

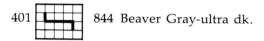

401   844 Beaver Gray-ultra dk.

Step Three: French Knots (one strand)

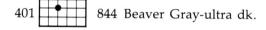

401   844 Beaver Gray-ultra dk.

Stitch Count: 62 × 41 (ship)

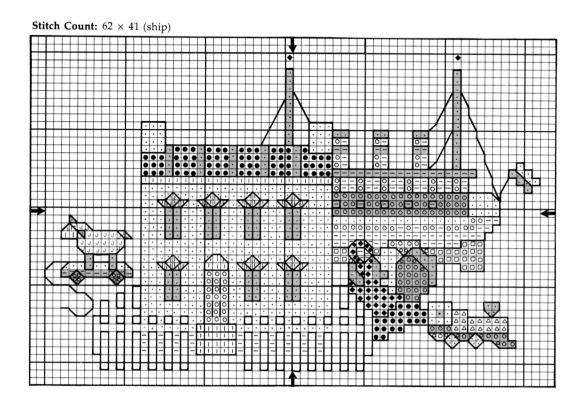

Stitch Count: 61 × 64 (horse)

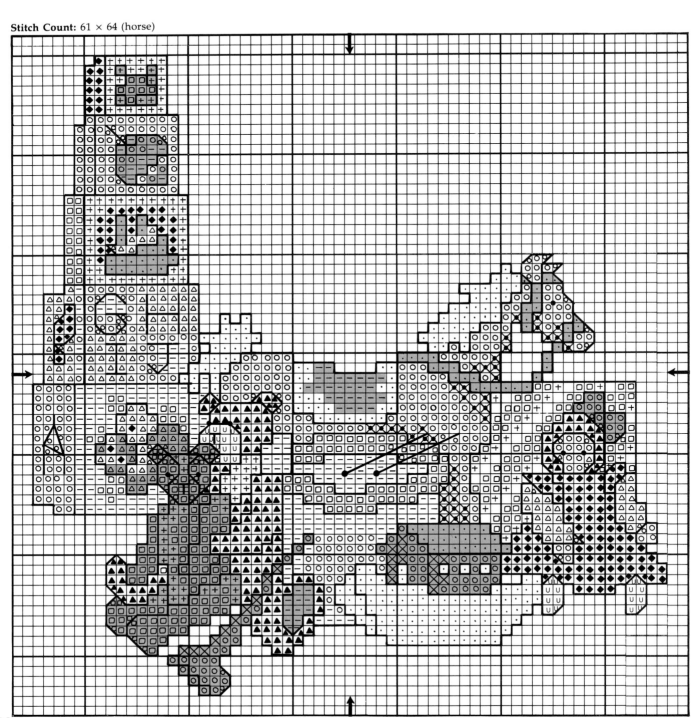

MATERIALS for ruffle band stocking

Completed cross-stitch on yellow Dublin Linen 25
¾ yard of light blue print fabric; matching thread
½ yard of pink print fabric
Scraps of fabric in various colors for patches
1¼ yard of ¼"–wide pink ribbon
2 ½"–wide green buttons
DMC floss (347)
Tracing paper
Dressmakers' pen

DIRECTIONS

All seam allowances are ¼".

1. Make pattern for stocking. Place pattern over the design piece with the center of design 5" from top and 3¼" from sides. Cut out. From scraps of fabric cut one 1" × 7½" strip and five triangular patches of various sizes.

2. Match top edge of 1" × 7½" strip to top edge of stocking. Turn lower edge under ¼" and slipstitch. Cut one 7½" piece of pink ribbon. Slipstitch below strip. Turn patch edges under ¼" and slipstitch to design piece; see photo for placement. Sew a half fern stitch with floss around edges of heel patch. Sew buttons 1" from bottom edge of design.

3. From pink print fabric, cut 4"–wide strips on the bias to equal 44" for ruffle. From blue print fabric, cut four stocking pieces according to pattern and one 2" × 4" strip for loop. Mark 1¼" inside the edge of stocking front piece. Cut on marking lines to make front border piece.

4. Turn inside edges of border piece under ¼" and pin to design piece. Slipstitch around inside edges. Clip corners and turn border out. Then fern stitch with floss around inside of border beginning and ending at ribbon.

5. Fold the 2" × 4" loop strip to measure 1" × 4". Stitch the long edge. Turn. Topstitch both long edges. Fold in half with raw ends together and pin to the top right side seam.

6. Stitch stocking front and back pieces with right sides together. Clip curves. Turn. Set aside.

7. With right sides of lining front and back pieces together, stitch leaving the top open and an opening in the seam above the heel. Clip curves.

8. Fold ruffle to measure 2" × 44". Stitch gathering threads on open edge. Gather to fit top edge of stocking. Turn ends under and stitch. Match and stitch top edges of ruffle and stocking with right sides together.

9. Slide lining over stocking with right sides together and the ruffle sandwiched between. Match side seams and stitch top edge. Turn the stocking through the opening. Slipstitch opening closed. Tuck lining inside the stocking.

10. Cut remaining ribbon into one 10" and one 26" strip. Fold 10" strip in half and tack center to right side of ribbon strip on stocking front. Tie a bow with 4" loops. Tack bow on top of 10" strip.

MATERIALS for maroon band stocking

Completed cross-stitch on yellow Dublin Linen 25
¾ yard blue print fabric; matching thread
¼ yard maroon fabric; matching thread
Scraps of fabric in various colors for patches
2 ½"–wide blue/white buttons
1 yard cording
Paper for pattern
Dressmakers' pen

DIRECTIONS

All seam allowances are ¼".

1. Make pattern for stocking. Place pattern over the design piece with the center of design 6¾" from top and 3¾" from sides. Cut out. From scraps of fabric cut one 1" × 6" strip and five triangular patches of various sizes and colors. From maroon fabric cut one 2" × 7¼" strip and one 2" × 4" strip for loop. Cut 1"–wide bias strips, piecing as needed, to measure 1 yard. Make 1 yard of corded piping. Set aside.

2. Place 1" × 6" strip 2¼" from top of design piece. Turn lower edge under ¼" and slipstitch. Match raw edge of 2" × 7¼" strip with top edge of design piece. Turn lower edge under ¼" and slipstitch over top of 1" × 6" strip. Turn patch edges under ¼" and slipstitch to design piece; see photo for placement. Sew buttons 3" from the top and 2" from each side of design piece.

3. From blue print fabric, cut four stocking pieces. Mark 1¼" inside the edge of stocking front piece. Cut on marking lines to make front border piece.

4. Turn insides edges of border piece under ¼" and pin to design piece. Slipstitch around inside edges.

5. Stitch piping around sides and bottom of right side of design piece. Stitch the stocking front and back pieces with right sides together sewing on stitching line of piping. Clip curves. Turn. Set aside.

6. Stitch lining front and back pieces with right sides together leaving the top open and an opening in the side seam above the heel. Clip curves.

7. Fold the 2" × 4" loop strip to measure 1" × 4". Stitch the long edge. Turn. Topstitch both long edges. Fold in half with raw ends together and pin to the top right side seam.

8. Slide lining over stocking with right sides together. Match side seams and stitch top edge. Turn the stocking through the opening. Slipstitch opening closed. Tuck lining inside the stocking.

MATERIALS for blue band stocking

Completed cross-stitch on yellow Dublin Linen 25
½ yard of red print fabric; matching thread
Scraps of blue print fabric
Scraps of fabric in various colors for patches
3 assorted buttons
1¾ yards cording
Dressmakers' pen

DIRECTIONS

1. Make pattern for stocking. Cut the design piece 5½" × 7" with the design centered. From the blue print fabric, cut one 1¾" × 7½" strip. Cut four stocking pieces from red print fabric according to pattern.* Also cut one 2" × 4" strip for loop and 1"–wide bias, piecing as needed, to equal 1¾ yards. Make 1¾ yards of corded piping.

2. Mark heel and toe placement on stocking front piece. Stitch scraps together in crazy-quilting fashion to cover heel and toe area; see photo. Fold under raw edges and slipstitch in place.

3. Match blue print strip to top edge of right side of design piece. Stitch. Match top edges of blue print strip* and stocking front piece.* Turn lower edge of design piece under ¼" and slipstitch.

4. Cut one 42" piece of piping and stitch to stocking front piece. Stitch the stocking front and back pieces with right sides together sewing on stitching line of the piping. Clip curves and turn. Set aside.

5. Stitch the lining front and back pieces with right sides together leaving the top edge open and an opening in the side seam above the heel. Clip curves.

6. Fold the 2" × 4" loop strip to measure 1" × 4". Stitch the long edge. Turn. Topstitch both long edges. Fold in half with raw ends together and pin to the top right side seam.

7. Stitch the remaining length of piping around the top edge of the stocking catching loop in seam. Slide lining over stocking with right sides together, matching side seams. Stitch top edges on the stitching line of piping. Turn the stocking through the opening. Slipstitch opening closed. Tuck lining inside the stocking.

* Note: the wrong side of the fabric will serve as the right side. The effect is a soft, worn appearance.

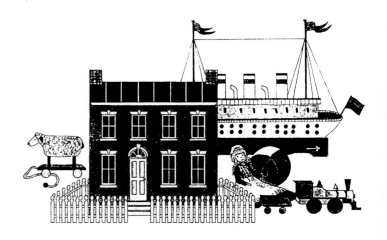

1 square = 1"

1 square = 1"

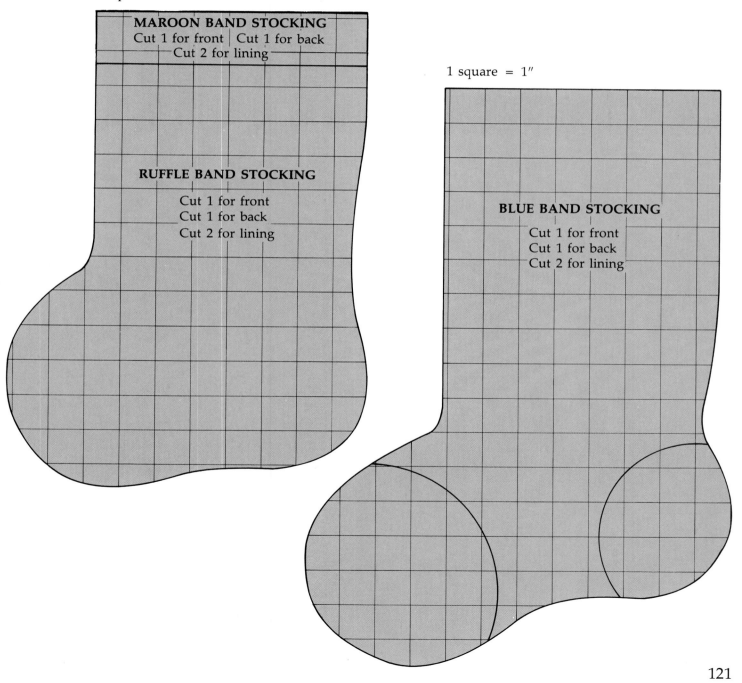

MAROON BAND STOCKING
Cut 1 for front | Cut 1 for back
Cut 2 for lining

RUFFLE BAND STOCKING

Cut 1 for front
Cut 1 for back
Cut 2 for lining

BLUE BAND STOCKING

Cut 1 for front
Cut 1 for back
Cut 2 for lining

Stitch Count: 16 × 22 (doll)

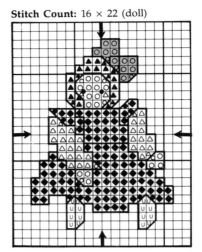

FOUR ORNAMENTS

Stitched on ivory Linda 27 over two threads, the
finished design size for the doll is 1⅛″ × 1⅝″; the
garland is 2¾″ × 1¾″; the blocks are ⅞″ × 1¾″;
and the jester is 1½″ × 1¾″. The fabric was cut
12″ × 4″ for each design.

Step One: Cross-stitch (two strands)

ANCHOR			DMC (used for sample)	
886	−	◿	677	Old Gold-vy. lt.
891	○	◿	676	Old Gold-lt.
323	○	◿	721	Orange Spice-med.
324	□	◿	922	Copper-lt.
339	+		920	Copper-med.
9	△	◿	760	Salmon
11	−	◿	3328	Salmon-med.
13	·		347	Salmon-dk.
920	◆	◿	932	Antique Blue-lt.
921	·		931	Antique Blue-med.
843	+	◿	3364	Pine Green
216	□	◿	367	Pistachio Green-dk.
378	U	◿	841	Beige Brown-lt.
380	▲	◿	839	Beige Brown-dk.

Stitch Count: 37 × 23 (garland)

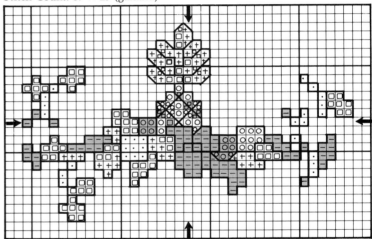

Step Two: Backstitch (one strand)

401		844 Beaver Gray-ultra dk.

Step Three: French Knots (one strand)

401		844 Beaver Gray-ultra dk.

Stitch Count: 12 × 23 (blocks)

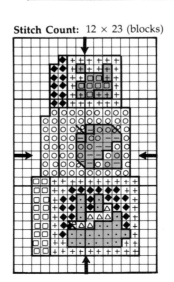

Stitch Count: 21 × 24 (jester)

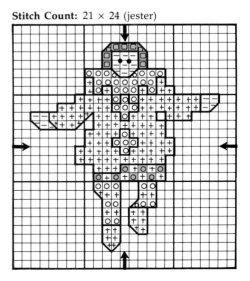

MATERIALS for one ornament

Completed cross-stitch on ivory Linda 27
One 7″ × 7″ piece of ivory fabric
One 3″ Styrofoam ball
6″ of ivory cord
Small paring knife
Glue
Pins
9″ of live ivy or holly

DIRECTIONS Ornament with design on front

1. Mark the center top and center bottom of the Styrofoam ball. Score a vertical circle around the ball with knife.

2. Center the design on the front panel. Pin the design piece to the ball.

3. Poke the fabric into the score line with paring knife. Take small tucks as needed to mold the fabric over the round surface. Keep the score line as narrow and inconspicuous as possible. Trim excess fabric close to the ball. Attach ivory fabric in same way.

4. Cut a 6″ piece of cord. Fold the cord to make a 3″ loop. Poke a hole in the top of the ornament. Glue both ends of the cord into the hole.

5. Place the ivy or holly over the score line. Glue and pin as needed to secure.

Ornament with design band

1. Mark the center top and center bottom of the Styrofoam ball. Score a circle around ball ½″ below top and ½″ above bottom with knife.

2. Center the design between score marks. Pin the stitched piece to the ball.

3. Cut two 3½″ × 3½″ pieces from ivory fabric. Repeat Step 3 above to cover the top and bottom of ornament.

4. Repeat Steps 4 and 5 above.

SLEEPING BEAUTY

Sleeping Beauty will rest in style in this gorgeous royal gown adorned with a colorful cross-stitch border. In her elegant attire, she awaits her Prince's awakening kiss. Instructions for her gown are found on page 140.

Meagan's storybook collection reflects the dreams of a childhood filled with magic, drama and adventure. She relives her favorite fairy tales by dressing up in a wardrobe of eight fanciful dresses adorned with cross-stitch. These never-never-land styles are irresistible to any girl – young or old.

DOLL BODY

MATERIALS for doll body

Porcelain doll parts
⅛ yard of white fabric; matching thread
Stuffing
Glue
Dressmakers' pen

DIRECTIONS

All seam allowances are ¼".

1. Cut out all body pieces according to patterns.

2. With right sides together, fold one arm piece and stitch the outside edges, leaving the bottom edge open. Turn and stuff. At the opening, turn fabric under ¼". Insert a porcelain arm; glue. Repeat for second arm.

3. To make legs, fold one leg piece and stitch the outside edges, leaving the top and bottom edges open. Turn. At the bottom opening, turn fabric under ¼". Insert a porcelain leg; glue. Stuff. Repeat for second leg.

4. Sew darts in the body pieces. With right sides together, stitch front and back along the side edges of body piece, leaving bottom open.

5. With the body piece wrong side out, place the legs inside the body so that the raw edges on the legs align with the raw edges on the bottom of the body. Sew across the bottom front only, securing legs. Turn. Stuff firmly. Slipstitch opening closed.

6. Tack the arms to the body at the shoulders. Glue the head to the top of the body.

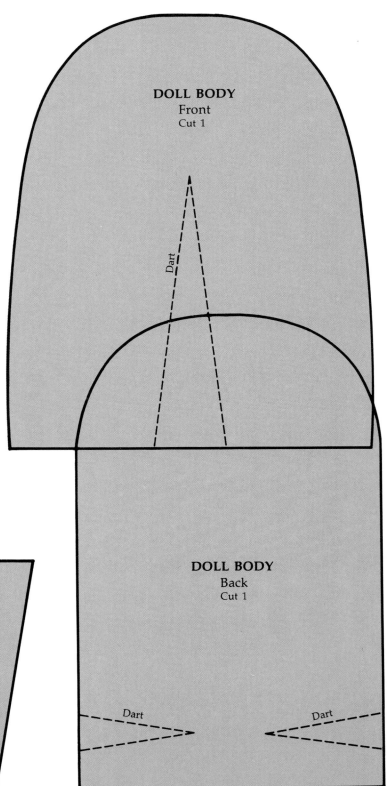

DOLL BODY
Front
Cut 1

Dart

DOLL BODY
Back
Cut 1

Dart   Dart

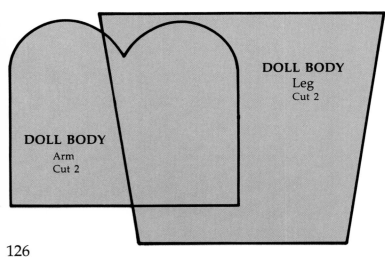

DOLL BODY
Leg
Cut 2

DOLL BODY
Arm
Cut 2

BASIC DRESS

MATERIALS for one dress

¼ yard of 45″–wide fabric; matching thread
Two small snap sets
6″–8″ of elastic thread
Dressmakers' pen

DIRECTIONS

All seam allowances are ¼″.

1. Cut one 6½″ × 22″ piece for the skirt. Cut the bodice front, bodice back and sleeves according to patterns.

2. With right sides of one bodice front and two bodice back pieces together, stitch the shoulders. Repeat for the remaining bodice front and bodice back pieces.

3. Place right sides of the two bodices together, matching shoulder seams. Stitch along one center back seam, around the neck, and the second center back. Clip the curved edges. Turn right side out. Proceed to handle both layers of the bodice as one layer of fabric.

4. Stitch a ⅛″–wide hem in the wrist edge of one

sleeve. Stitch gathering threads in sleeve cap. Gather the sleeve to fit the armhole. Stitch the sleeve cap to the bodice. Repeat.

5. With right sides together, stitch one side seam and one sleeve. Repeat for the remaining side seam and sleeve. Sew elastic thread ¼″ above the hem at the wrist, either by hand or with zigzag stitch over thread. Gather to fit the doll and secure.

6. Fold the skirt with right sides together and stitch the short ends together to within 2″ of the top edge; backstitch. (This seam is the center back; the long edge with the opening will be the waist.) Fold the edges of the waist opening double to the wrong side and stitch with a narrow hem.

7. Mark the center front of the skirt. Stitch gathering threads along the waist edge. Fold ½″ hem double to the wrong side along the lower edge of the skirt. Hem by hand or machine.

8. Mark the center front of the bodice at the waist. Gather the skirt to fit the bodice. With right sides together, match the center of the skirt to the center of the bodice and stitch.

9. Sew snaps on the center back opening at neck and waist of dress.

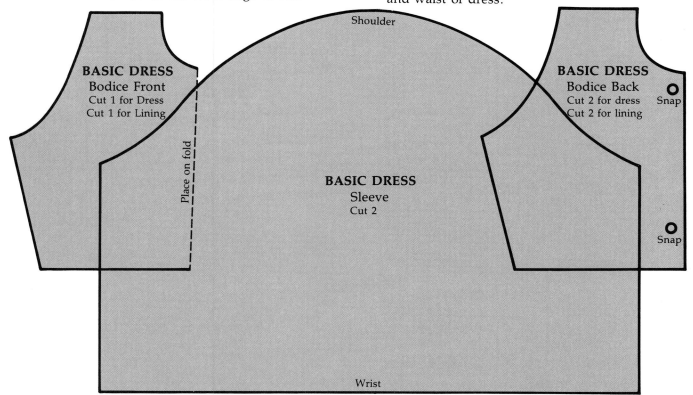

PANTALOONS

MATERIALS for pantaloons
¼ yard of lightweight fabric; matching thread
3″ of ⅛″–wide elastic
6″–8″ of elastic thread
Dressmakers' pen

DIRECTIONS

All seam allowances are ⅛″.

1. Cut the pantaloon pieces according to pattern. (The pantaloons for "Alice in Wonderland" are 1″ shorter than the others.)

2. With right sides together, stitch the center front and center back seams. Then stitch the inseam.

3. Fold ½″ to the wrong side at the waist. Turn under the raw edge and stitch to make the casing, leaving an opening. Thread the elastic through the casing. Overlap the ends ½″ and secure. Slipstitch the casing closed.

4. Stitch a narrow hem in each leg. Sew elastic thread ½″ above the hem, either by hand or with zigzag stitch over elastic. Gather to fit the doll and secure.

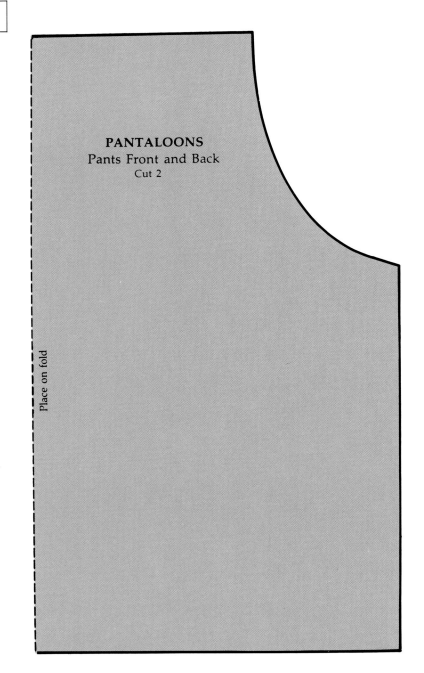

PANTALOONS
Pants Front and Back
Cut 2

Place on fold

MATERIALS for smock

¼ yard of cracked wheat Murano 30 (includes completed cross-stitch design); matching thread
¼ yard of cream fabric for lining
One hook and eye
Dressmakers' pen

DIRECTIONS

All seam allowances are ¼".

1. Cut the design piece for front according to pattern. From the unstitched Murano, cut the back pieces for smock and a 1"–wide bias, piecing as needed, to equal 6". Then cut front and back pieces from lining fabric.

2. Stitch shoulder seams of smock. Then stitch the side seams. Repeat with lining pieces.

3. Place right sides of smock and lining together matching the side and shoulder seams. Stitch the center back seams leaving a small opening to turn through. Turn. Slipstitch the opening closed.

4. Fold the raw edges to inside around armholes and slipstitch closed.

5. Handling smock and lining as one piece of fabric, stitch gathering threads around neck. Gather neckline to fit bias, placing all fullness near the center front. With right sides together, stitch bias around neck. Fold double to the wrong side and slipstitch. Fold raw edges of bias to inside on ends and slipstitch closed.

6. Sew the hook and eye to the neck at the center back.

MARY HAD A LITTLE LAMB

The heart motifs are the top left and right hearts on **Spring Bouquet**. Stitched on cracked wheat Murano 30 over two threads, the finished design size is 5" × 1⅜". The fabric was cut 10" × 8". The stitch count is 75 × 21. Her smock is worn over a peach **Basic Dress**.

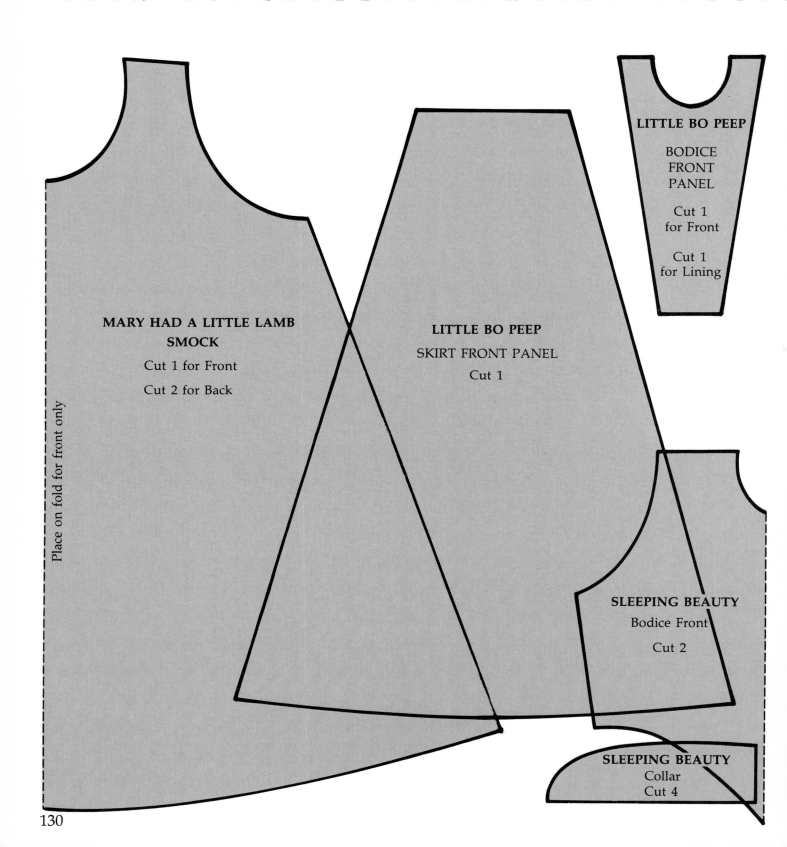

LITTLE BO PEEP

BODICE
FRONT
PANEL

Cut 1
for Front

Cut 1
for Lining

**MARY HAD A LITTLE LAMB
SMOCK**

Cut 1 for Front

Cut 2 for Back

LITTLE BO PEEP

SKIRT FRONT PANEL

Cut 1

Place on fold for front only

SLEEPING BEAUTY

Bodice Front

Cut 2

SLEEPING BEAUTY
Collar
Cut 4

CINDERELLA

The left bird patch was stitched on tan Jobelan 28; the mouse patch on teal Jobelan 28; and the right bird patch on cream Jobelan 28. All designs were stitched over two threads. The finished design size for the largest patch is 1″ × 1″. The fabric was cut 2″ × 2″ for each design.

MATERIALS for dress, scarf and apron
Completed cross-stitch on Jobelan 28 (see sample information); brown thread
¼ yard of antique blue fabric for skirt and scarf
⅛ yard of cream fabric for bodice; matching thread
¼ yard of tan fabric for apron
Two small snap sets
6″–8″ of elastic thread
Dressmakers' pen

DIRECTIONS

All seam allowances are ¼″.

1. Trim completed design pieces to 1½″ × 1½″. From tan fabric, cut one 24″ × 5½″ piece for apron skirt and one 1½″ × 17½″ piece for waistband.

2. From blue fabric, cut one 6½″ × 27″ piece for the skirt and one 7″ × 7″ square for scarf. From cream fabric, cut the bodice front, bodice back and sleeves according to **Basic Dress** patterns. Complete Steps 2-9 of **Basic Dress**.

3. Turn edges of cross-stitched pieces under ¼″ on all edges; see photo for placement. Fern stitch (see diagram) to skirt.

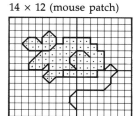

4. Mark centers of waistband piece and apron skirt. Stitch gathering threads in waist of skirt. Gather to 4″. Fold waistband piece in half and turn raw edges ⅜″ to inside. Press. Sandwich skirt between waistband piece, matching center marks. Stitch long edge and ends of waistband.

5. Fold ½″ hem double to the wrong side along the lower edge of the apron skirt. Hem by hand or machine.

6. To finish bottom edge of skirt, cut three to four jagged edges through hem on each side of skirt.

Step One: Cross-stitch (two strands)
ANCHOR   DMC (used for sample)

ANCHOR		DMC
891		676 Old Gold-lt.
9		760 Salmon
920		932 Antique Blue-lt.
921		931 Antique Blue-med.
246		319 Pistachio Green-vy. dk.
8581		3023 Brown Gray-lt.

Step Two: Backstitch (one strand)

401		844 Beaver Gray-ultra dk.

Stitch Count: 14 × 14 (left and right patches)
14 × 12 (mouse patch)

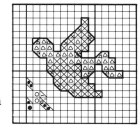
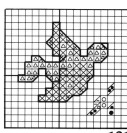

WIZARD OF OZ

The designs are taken from **Letters from the Heart**. The basket of apples is underneath the A. The border is repeated around the bottom of skirt and on bib. Stitched on Waste Canvas 14 over one thread, the fabric was cut 28″ × 6″ and the Waste Canvas was cut 28″ × 2½″. Stitch 26″ of border 1″ from bottom edge of dress with basket of apples centered and sitting on top of border. Then stitch 2″ of blue border for bib of dress with scrap of Waste Canvas.

MATERIALS for dress

¼ yard of light blue fabric (includes cross-stitch piece for skirt and bib); matching thread

⅛ yard of white fabric; matching thread

Two small snap sets

6″–8″ of elastic thread

Dressmakers' pen

DIRECTIONS

All seam allowances are ¼″.

1. For bib front, trim the 3″ × 3″ design piece to 2″ × 2¼″ with border horizontal and center of design ½″ from top edge. From unstitched blue fabric, cut a 2″ × 2¼″ piece for bib lining and two ¾″ × 4″ strips for straps. From white fabric, cut the bodice front, bodice back and sleeves according to **Basic Dress** patterns.

2. Complete Steps 2–7 of **Basic Dress** using the 28″ × 6″ completed cross-stitch design piece as skirt.

3. Fold strap pieces to measure ⅜″ × 4″. Stitch the long edge and turn. Sandwich one end of each strap, ¼″ from each outside edge, between bib front and lining with right sides together. Stitch across the top edge, securing strap ends; then stitch each side. Turn.

4. Mark the center front of the skirt. Stitch gathering threads along the waist edge. Fold ½″ hem double to the wrong side along the lower edge of the skirt. Hem by hand or machine.

5. Mark the center front of the bodice at the waist. Gather the skirt to fit the bodice. Match the center of the skirt to the center of the bib piece with right sides together. Then, with right sides of the skirt and bodice together and bib piece sandwiched between, match the centers and stitch.

6. Sew snap sets on the center back opening at neck and waist of dress.

7. Turn ends of straps under ¼″ and stitch to waist edge of dress ½″ from each side of center back seam.

LITTLE RED RIDING HOOD

The design is the small middle border on the right side of **Bless This House**. Stitched on dawn gray damask Aida 14 over one thread, the finished design size is 4¾" × 1⅛". The fabric was cut 14" × 7". The stitch count is 67 × 16.

MATERIALS for jumper

Completed cross-stitch on dawn gray damask Aida
   14 (see sample information); matching thread
¼ yard of red print fabric; matching thread
¼ yard of ¹/₁₆"–wide red satin ribbon
Large needle

DIRECTIONS

All seam allowances are ¼".

1. To make apron, trim design piece to 13" × 6" with center of design 1⅝" from bottom edge. Hem side and bottom edges of design piece. Mark the center front at top edge.

2. From red print fabric, cut a 30" × 6½" piece for skirt. Then cut only jumper front and back pieces according to patterns.

3. With right sides of one jumper front and two jumper back pieces together, stitch the shoulders and side seams. Repeat for the remaining jumper front and jumper back pieces.

4. Place right sides of the two jumper pieces together, matching shoulder seams. Stitch along one center back seam, around the neck, and the second center back. Clip the curved edges. Turn right side out. Fold the raw edges of armholes to inside and slipstitch closed. Proceed to handle both layers of the jumper as one layer of fabric.

5. Fold the skirt with right sides together and stitch the short ends together within 2" of the top edge; backstitch. (This seam is the center back; the long edge with the opening will be the waist.) Fold the edges of the waist opening double to the wrong side and stitch with a narrow hem.

6. Mark the center front of the skirt. Match design piece and pin together. Stitch gathering threads along the waist edge. Fold ½" hem double to the wrong side along the lower edge of the skirt. Hem by hand or machine.

7. Mark the center front of the jumper at the waist. Gather the skirt to fit the jumper. Match the center of the skirt to the center of the design piece with right sides of both facing up. Then, with right sides of the apron/skirt and jumper together, match the centers and stitch. Zigzag over raw edges of all layers.

8. Sew snaps on the center back opening at neck and waist of dress.

9. Mark placement for lacing on jumper front according to pattern. Using the large needle, begin stitching on the front side at upper left mark and leaving a 3" tail of ribbon. See diagram for stitching sequence.

MATERIALS for blouse

⅛ yard of white fabric; matching thread
Two small snaps
6–8" of elastic thread
Dressmakers' pen

DIRECTIONS

All seam allowances are ⅛".

1. To make patterns for blouse, extend the lower edge of bodice front and bodice back pieces of **Basic Dress** by 1". Cut bodice front, bodice back and sleeve pieces for front and lining according to patterns.

2. Complete Steps 2-5 of **Basic Dress**.

3. Hem bottom edge of blouse. Sew snaps on the center back opening at the neck and 1" below the neck.

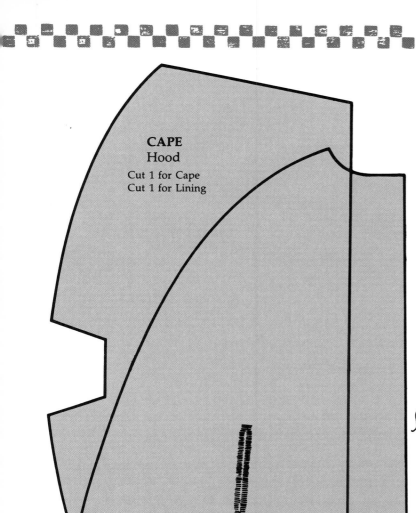

CAPE
Hood
Cut 1 for Cape
Cut 1 for Lining

CAPE
Front and Back
Cut 2 for Cape Front
Cut 1 on fold for Cape Back
Cut 2 for Cape Front Lining
Cut 1 on fold for Cape Back Lining

MATERIALS for cape

¼ yard of red fabric; matching thread
1 yard of ¹/₁₆″–wide red satin ribbon

DIRECTIONS

All seam allowances are ¼″.

1. Cut cape hood and cape front and back pieces from red fabric according to patterns.

2. Fold hood piece on center mark with right sides together. Stitch seam in center back; see diagram. Refold with center mark matching center back seam. Stitch the horizontal seam; see diagram. Repeat with hood lining.

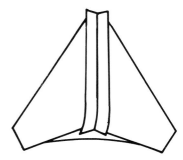

3. Stitch cape front pieces to cape back on side seams. Repeat for lining.

4. Mark center back of neckline. Match center back to seam in hood. Stitch hood to cape. Repeat for lining.

5. Match edges of cape and lining with right sides together. Stitch outside edges of cape, leaving a small opening in bottom edge. Clip corners. Turn. Slipstitch opening closed.

6. Make buttonholes; see pattern for placement. (These are the openings for each arm.)

7. Cut ribbon into two equal lengths. Fold one length in half and tack fold to make a small loop on seam which joins hood and cape.

ALICE IN WONDERLAND

The design is taken from the center block on **The Comforter**. The cat in the basket and flowers are used; see photo. Stitched with Waste Canvas 14 over one thread, the finished design size is 3½" × 1⅝". The fabric was cut 24" × 6" and the Waste Canvas was cut 4" × 2½". The stitch count is 49 × 22.

MATERIALS for apron and dress

¼ yard of white fabric (includes cross-stitch piece for skirt); matching thread
¼ yard of royal blue and white fabric; matching thread
Five small snap sets
6"–8" of elastic thread
Dressmakers' pen

DIRECTIONS

All seam allowances are ¼".

1. From blue fabric, cut one 33" × 5" piece for the skirt. Then cut the bodice front, bodice back and sleeves according to **Basic Dress** patterns. Complete Steps 2–9 of **Basic Dress**.

2. Trim completed cross-stitch piece to 22" × 4½" with center of design 1¾" from bottom. From remaining white fabric, cut ruffles according to pattern and two 1¾" × 2" pieces for bib front and lining. Then cut four ¾" × 5" strips for straps and two ¾" × 8" strips for waistband.

3. With right sides of bib front and lining together, stitch across the top edge. Fold right side out. Sandwich one edge of bib between the right sides of two strap pieces with bottom edges aligned. Stitch entire long edge of strap securing bib. Repeat with remaining strap pieces, securing second edge of bib.

4. Make a narrow hem in curved edge of one ruffle piece. Stitch gathering threads in straight edges of ruffle piece. Gather ruffle pieces to 4½". Place ruffle and shoulder strap with right sides together, placing ruffle ¼" from bottom edge of bib front. Fold raw ends of ruffle and edges of strap to the inside and slipstitch. Repeat with other ruffle piece.

5. Mark centers of bib and both long edges of ¾" × 8" strips for waistband. Sandwich bib between two waistband pieces with right sides together, matching center marks. Stitch long edge and ends of waistband. Turn waistband down with right sides out.

6. Stitch gathering threads in waist of skirt. Turn. Gather to same size as waistband. Stitch skirt to waistband with right sides together. Zigzag over raw edges of all layers.

7. Fold ½" hem double to the wrong side along the lower edge of the skirt. Hem by hand or machine.

8. Sew a snap set to ends of waistband. Then sew remaining snap sets ¼" from each waistband snap and to ends of straps. (Straps are crisscrossed when doll is dressed.)

LITTLE BO PEEP

The floral design is the center basket of flowers on **Garden in the Park**. Stitched on pink Dublin Linen 25 over two threads, the finished design size is 2⅝" × 3¼". The fabric was cut 7" × 8". The stitch count is 33 × 41.

MATERIALS for one dress
Completed cross-stitch on pink Dublin Linen 25 (see sample information)
¼ yard of white and pink striped fabric; matching thread
½ yard of white satin corded piping
Two small snap sets
6"–8" of elastic thread
Dressmakers' pen

DIRECTIONS

All seam allowances are ¼".

1. Center and cut design piece according to skirt front panel pattern*, with center of design 2½" from bottom edge. From linen scraps, cut bodice front panel pieces according to pattern*.

2. From striped fabric, cut one 28½" × 6½" piece for the skirt and cut peplum and bodice front panel (for lining) according to patterns. Then cut the bodice front, bodice back and sleeves according to **Basic Dress** patterns.

3. Stitch piping to each side of the bodice front panel. Stitch design piece and lining piece on stitching line of piping with right sides together. Turn. Pin panel to the center and right side of one bodice front.

4. Complete Steps 2 - 5 of **Basic Dress** securing panel in neckline seam.

5. Center and pin the skirt front panel design piece on top of the striped skirt piece. Trace the sides. Cut on lines and discard center striped panel. Stitch the piping to each side of the design piece. Then with right sides of design piece and skirt piece together, stitch on stitching line of piping. Repeat for second side.

6. Fold the skirt with right sides together and stitch the short ends together to within 2" of the top edge; backstitch. (This seam is the center back; the long edge with the opening will be the waist.) Fold the edges of the waist opening double to the wrong side and stitch with a narrow hem.

7. With right sides of peplum pieces together, stitch the center back ends together to within 2" of the top edge; backstitch. Make a narrow hem in the curved edge.

8. Place peplum piece over skirt piece and pin with ends of peplum at cording. Stitch gathering threads through both layers along the waist edge.

9. Mark the center front of the bodice at the waist. Gather the skirt/peplum to fit the bodice. Then, with right sides of the skirt and bodice together, match the centers. Stitch. Zigzag over raw edges of all layers.

10. Sew snaps on the center back opening at neck and waist of dress.

* Patterns are on page 130.

turquoise piece for other side. Using this as the bodice front piece, center the design and cut the bodice front, bodice back and sleeves according to **Basic Dress** patterns.

3. Complete Steps 2 - 5 of **Basic Dress**.

4. Fold the 28″ × 3″ design piece in half to measure 28″ × 1½″. Zigzag the long edge. Then stitch the design piece to the bottom edge of the skirt with right sides together.

5. Fold skirt with right sides together and stitch the short ends together within 2″ of the top edge; backstitch. (This seam is the center back; the long edge with the opening will be the waist.) Fold the edges of the waist opening double to the wrong side and stitch with a narrow hem.

6. Mark the center front of the skirt and stitch gathering threads in waist. Then mark the center front of the bodice at the waist. Gather the skirt to fit the bodice. With right sides together, match the centers and stitch. Zigzag over raw edges of all layers.

7. Sew snaps on the center back opening at neck and waist of dress.

LITTLE MISS MUFFET

Stitched on white Murano 30 over two threads, the finished design size for each motif is 2⅝″ × 1″. The fabric was cut 28″ × 2″. Leave ½″ between motifs. Stitch one basket design for top of dress.

MATERIALS for dress
Completed cross-stitch pieces on Murano 30 (see sample information)
¼ yard of turquoise fabric; matching thread
Two small snap sets
6″–8″ of elastic thread
Dressmakers' pen

DIRECTIONS

All seam allowances are ¼″.

1. Trim completed cross-stitch piece for bodice to 1½″ × 2¼″ with design centered. From turquoise fabric, cut two 2″ × 3″ pieces for bodice front and one 4½″ × 27″ piece for the skirt.

2. With right sides of bodice design and one 2″ × 3″ piece of turquoise fabric together, match the lower edges and stitch the side seam. Repeat with second

Step One: Cross-stitch (one strand)
ANCHOR   DMC (used for sample)

Anchor	Symbol	DMC	Color
9	−	760	Salmon
11	o	3328	Salmon-med.
22	●	816	Garnet
167	∴	597	Turquoise
843	□	3364	Pine Green
216	▲	367	Pistachio Green-dk.
341	✕	919	Red Copper

Stitch Count: 39 × 15 (one motif)

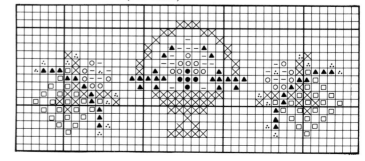

138

SLEEPING BEAUTY

Stitched on ivory Linda 27 over two threads, the finished design size is 2⅞″ × ⅞″. The fabric was cut 7″ × 23″. Begin stitching bird motif on left side of fabric with center of design 2″ from bottom edge. Alternate flower and bird motifs leaving ⅜″ between.

MATERIALS

¼ yard of ivory Linda 27 (includes cross-stitched piece for skirt); matching thread
Two small snap sets
Dressmakers' pen
⅜ yard of ⅞″–wide gold trim for crown

DIRECTIONS

All seams are ¼″.

1. Cut bodice*, collar* and cuff pieces according to patterns. Then cut bodice back and sleeves (minus 1″ from bottom of sleeve) according to **Basic Dress** patterns.

2. Stitch right sides of two collar pieces together along the curved edge. Turn. Repeat with remaining pieces.

3. Complete Step 2 of **Basic Dress**. Match collar pieces at center front and baste to the right side of bodice front. Complete Step 3 of **Basic Dress**.

4. Stitch right sides of front and lining cuff pieces together leaving the long edge open. Turn.

5. Stitch gathering threads in sleeve caps and at the wrist edges. Gather wrist edge to fit cuff piece. With right sides of sleeve and cuff together, stitch the edge. Turn down.

6. Gather sleeve caps to fit armholes. Stitch the sleeve caps to the bodice. With right sides together, stitch one side seam and one sleeve to the cuff; backstitch. Repeat. Slipstitch the cuff side seam closed to fit wrist.

7. Fold skirt piece to measure 7″ × 11½″. (The fold is the center front). Cut a V-shape in the center front according to bottom of bodice pattern. Complete Step 6 of **Basic Dress**. Fold a ½″ hem to the wrong side of the skirt along the bottom edge of the skirt. Stitch hem by hand or machine.

8. Stitch gathering threads along waist edge of skirt. Pin the deepest point of V-shape in skirt to point of bodice front. Gather the skirt to fit the bodice. Stitch together.

9. Sew snap sets on the center back opening at the neck and waist of dress.

10. To make crown, cut one 7″ and one 4″ piece of gold trim. Place 7″ piece around head to fit and glue ends. Then glue 4″ piece behind crown in center front ½″ from bottom edge.

* Patterns are on page 130.

Step One: Cross-stitch (two strands)

ANCHOR   DMC (used for sample)

ANCHOR			DMC (used for sample)
323	O	◢	721 Orange Spice-med.
11	–	◢	3328 Salmon-med.
13	·	◢	347 Salmon-dk.
921	·	◢	931 Antique Blue-med.
216	▢		367 Pistachio Green-dk.

Step Two: Backstitch (one strand)

401		844 Beaver Gray-ultra dk.

Stitch Count: 39 × 12 (one motif)

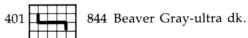

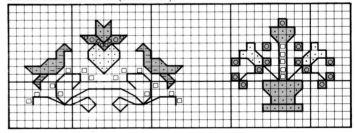

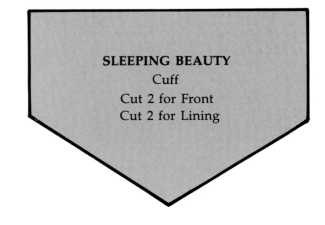

SLEEPING BEAUTY
Cuff
Cut 2 for Front
Cut 2 for Lining

CROSS-STITCH

Fabrics: Counted cross-stitch is usually worked on even-weave fabric. These fabrics are manufactured specifically for counted thread embroidery and are woven with the same number of vertical as horizontal threads per inch. Because the number of threads in the fabric is equal in each direction, each stitch will be the same size. It is the number of threads per inch in even-weave fabrics that determines the size of a finished design.

Other Fabrics: To determine the finished design size when using other fabrics, divide the threads per inch of the fabric into the vertical and horizontal stitch count of the design.

Waste Canvas: Cut the waste canvas 1" larger on all sides than the finished design size. Baste the waste canvas to the fabric to be stitched. Complete the stitching. When stitching is complete, dampen the stitched area with cold water. Pull the waste canvas threads out one at a time with tweezers. It is easier to pull all the threads running in one direction first, then pull out the opposite threads. Allow the stitching to dry. Place face down on a towel and iron.

Preparing Fabric: Cut even-weave fabric at least 3" larger on all sides than the design size or cut it the size specified in the sample paragraph. A 3" margin is the minimum amount of space that allows for working the edges of the design comfortably. If the item is to be finished into a sachet bag, for example, the fabric should be cut as directed. To keep fabric from fraying, whip stitch or machine zig zag the raw edges.

Needles: Needles should slip easily through the holes in the fabric but not pierce the fabric. Use a blunt tapestry needle, size 24 or 26. Never leave the needle in the design area of your work. It can leave rust or a permanent impression on your fabric.

Floss: All numbers and color names are cross referenced between ANCHOR and DMC brands of six-strand embroidery floss. Cut 18" lengths of floss. Run the floss over a damp sponge to straighten. Separate all six strands and use the number of strands called for in the code.

Centering Design: Find the center of the fabric by folding it in half horizontally and then vertically. Place a pin in the fold point to mark the center. Locate the center of the design on the graph by following vertical and horizontal arrows. Begin stitching at the center point of the graph and the fabric.

Securing the Floss: Start by inserting your needle up from the underside of the fabric at your starting point. Hold 1" of thread behind the fabric and stitch over it, securing with the first few stitches. To finish thread, run under four or more stitches on the back of the design. Never knot floss unless working on clothing.

Another method for securing floss is the waste knot. Knot your floss and insert your needle from the right side of the fabric about 1" from the design area. Work several stitches over the thread to secure. Cut off the knot later.

Stitching: For a smooth cross-stitch, use the "push and pull" method. Push the needle straight down and completely through fabric before pulling up. Do not pull the thread tight. The tension should be consistent throughout, making the stitches even. Make one stitch for every symbol on the chart. To stitch in rows, work from left to right and then back. Half-crosses are used to make a rounded shape. Make the longer stitch in the direction of the slanted line.

Carrying Floss: To carry floss, weave floss under the previously worked stitches on the back. Do not carry your thread across any fabric that is not or will not be stitched. Loose threads, especially dark ones, will show through the fabric.

Twisted Floss: If floss is twisted, drop the needle and allow the floss to unwind itself. Floss will cover best when lying flat. Use thread no longer than 18" because it will tend to twist and knot.

Cleaning Completed Work: When all stitching is complete, soak the completed work in cold water with a mild soap for 5 to 10 minutes. Rinse and roll work into a towel to remove excess water; do not wring. Place work face down on a dry towel and, with iron on a warm setting, iron until work is dry.

STITCHES

Cross-stitch: Make one cross for each symbol on the chart. Bring needle and thread up at A, down at B, up at C, and down again at D.

For rows, stitch from left to right, then back. All stitches should lie in the same direction.

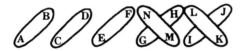

Half-cross: Make the longer stitch in the direction of the slanted line on the graph. The stitch actually fits three-fourths of the area. Bring needle and thread up at A, down at B, up at C, and down at D.

Backstitch: Complete all cross-stitching before working back stitches or other accent stitches. Working from left to right with one strand of floss (unless designated otherwise in code), bring needle and thread up at A, down at B, and up again at C. Going back down at A, continue in this manner.

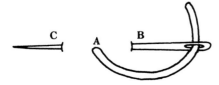

French Knot: Bring the needle up at A, using one strand of embroidery floss. Wrap floss around needle two times (unless indicated otherwise in instructions). Insert needle beside A, pulling floss until it fits snugly around needle. Pull needle through to back.

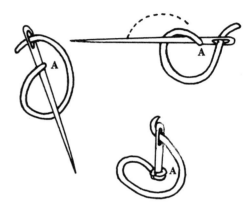

Beadwork: Attach beads to fabric with a half-cross, lower left to upper right. Secure beads by returning thread through beads, lower right to upper left. Complete row of half-crosses before returning to secure all beads.

Smyrna Cross: Make a cross-stitch over one square. Then work a horizontal stitch first and a vertical stitch over it to finish.

Long Loose Stitch: Secure thread by running ends through existing cross-stitch on back. Enter at point from wrong side of fabric and exit at end point. Secure ends.

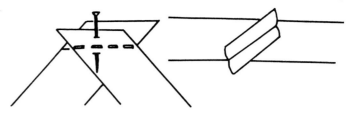

SEWING HINTS

Patterns: Use tracing paper to trace the patterns. Transfer all information. All patterns include seam allowance.

Clipping Seams: Clipping seam allowances is necessary on all curves, points, and most corners so that the finished seam will lie flat. Clip into the seam allowance at even intervals, ¼" to ½" apart, being careful not to cut through the stitching.

Slipstitch: Insert needle at A, slide it through the folded edge of the fabric for about ⅛" to ¼" and bring it out at B. Directly below B, take a small stitch through the second piece of fabric.

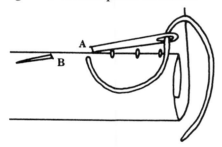

Gathering: Machine-stitch two parallel rows of long stitches ¼" and ½" from the edge of fabric (unless instructions say differently). Leave the ends of the thread 2" or 3" long. Pull the two bobbin threads and gather to fit the desired length. Long edges may need to be gathered from both ends. Disperse the fullness evenly and secure the threads in the seam by wrapping them around a pin in a figure eight.

Bias Strips: Bias strips are used for ruffles, binding, or corded piping. To cut bias, fold the fabric at a 45-degree angle to the grain of the fabric and crease. Cut on the crease. Cut additional strips the width indicated in instructions and parallel to the first cutting line. The ends of the bias strips should be on the grain of the fabric. Place the right sides of the ends together and stitch with a ¼"-seam. Continue to piece the strips until they are the length that is indicated in instructions.

Corded Piping: Piece bias strips together to equal the length needed for cording. Place the cord in the center of the wrong side of the strip and fold the fabric over it. Using a zipper foot, stitch close to the cord through both layers of fabric. Trim the seam allowance ¼" from the stitching line.

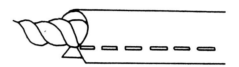

SUPPLIERS

All products are available retail from Shepherd's Bush, 220 24th Street, Ogden, UT 84401; 801-399-4546; or for a merchant near you, write the following suppliers:

Zweigart Fabrics:
Damask Aida 14 (Ivory)
Dublin Linen 25 (Sand, Yellow)
Linda 25 (Ivory)
Belfast Linen 32 (Cream, Driftwood)
Zweigart/Joan Toggit Ltd., 35 Fairfield Place, West Caldwell, NJ 07006

Meagan Porcelain Doll Parts
Chapelle Designers, Box 9252 Newgate Station, Ogden, UT 84409; (801) 621-2777

Footstool (Spring Bouquet)
Plain 'n' Fancy, P.O. Box 357, Mathews, VA 23109; (800) 327-7005

Clock
Wheatland Crafts, Route 5, Box 509, Simpsonville, SC 29681

Rocking Chair, Footstool (Two Houses)
Freeman Manufacturing, Inc., P.O. Box 382, Thomasville, NC 27388

Eyeglass Case, Makeup Pouch Hardware
Ghee's, 106 East Kings Highway, Suite 205, Shreveport, LA 71104

All of us at Sedgewood® Press are dedicated to offering you, our customer, the best books we can create. We are particularly concerned that all of the instructions for making projects are clear and accurate. Please address your correspondence to Customer Service Department, Sedgewood® Press, Meredith Corporation, 750 Third Avenue, New York NY 10017.

Country Cross-Stitch Designs: An American Sampler 1990 is the second in a series of cross-stitch books. If you would like the first book in the series, *Quilt Designs in Cross-Stitch: An American Sampler 1989,* please write to the address above.

For information on how you can have *Better Homes and Gardens* delivered to your door, write to: Mr. Robert Austin, P.O. Box 4536, Des Moines, IA 50336.

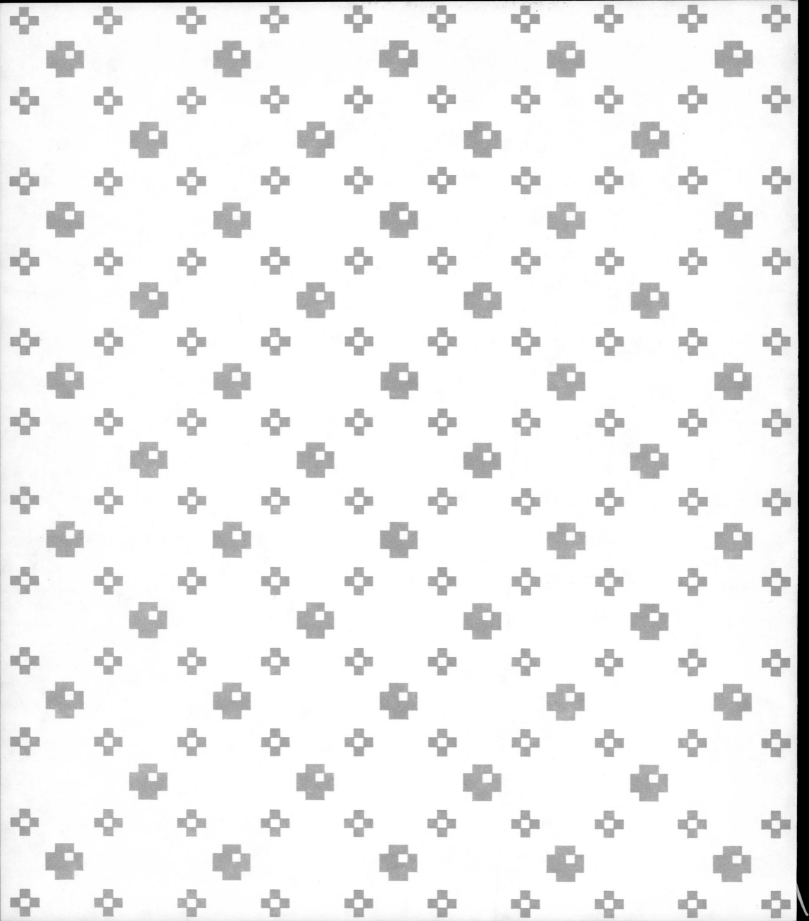